SELF LOVE

workbook for midlife
WOMEN
A 12-WEEK HEALING JOURNEY

Release Toxicity, Overcome Self-doubt, and Rediscover your TRUE WORTH..

© Copyright 2022 - All rights reserved.

The content contained within this book may not be reproduced, duplicated or transmitted without direct written permission from the author or the publisher.

Under no circumstances will any blame or legal responsibility be held against the publisher, or author, for any damages, reparation, or monetary loss due to the information contained within this book, either directly or indirectly.

Legal Notice:

This book is copyright protected. It is only for personal use. You cannot amend, distribute, sell, use, quote or paraphrase any part, or the content within this book, without the consent of the author or publisher.

Disclaimer Notice:

Please note the information contained within this document is for educational and entertainment purposes only. All effort has been executed to present accurate, up to date, reliable, complete information. No warranties of any kind are declared or implied.

Readers acknowledge that the author is not engaged in the rendering of legal, financial, medical or professional advice. The content within this book has been derived from various sources. Please consult a licensed professional before attempting any techniques outlined in this book.

By reading this document, the reader agrees that under no circumstances is the author responsible for any losses, direct or indirect, that are incurred as a result of the use of the information contained within this document, including, but not limited to, errors, omissions, or inaccuracies.

ISBN:

$129 FREE

Achieve a Worry-Free Smile with these
12 Mental Health Books!

The Easy Way to Improve Mental Health

Therapy doesn't have to be so expensive and complicated. That's why we are giving you these 7 eBooks and 5 bonus workbooks so you can start improving your mental health right away, without leaving your home!

- **Stop Worrying All the Time**: Stop those nagging thoughts in their tracks with mindfulness and anti-anxiety tips expert CBT therapists use!
- **Do Therapy Your Way**: Start taking action with 5 BONUS workbooks, so you can start smiling, laughing, and enjoying life on your own!
- **Love Yourself, Love Others**: Enhance your career, relationships, hobbies, and more as you march through each day with confident self-esteem

Scan to download:

Table Of Contents

Introduction 1

    The Best Time for Self-Renewal Is Midlife 3

    Self-Love: The Best Form of Healing...3

    Embrace the Magic in Every Step 4

    Let's Aim to Beat the Negative Factors Associated With Midlife..........5

    My Objective Is to Help You Heal 6

    Summary of Chapters..7

Chapter 1: Understanding the True Power of Self-Love 9

    What Is Self-Love? 9

    It Is Time to Love Yourself...12

    Self-Love Versus Self-Hate..12

    Monitoring Your Negative Thoughts..13

    Alison's Lesson in Self-Love 16

    Choosing Self-Love Is the Happy Ending You Need...........................17

    The Importance of Self-Love for Midlife Women 21

    How to Deal With Moments of Regret...22

    You Can Change Anything in Your Life..23

    Start a Healing Journal 24

    Explore Yourself More: Let's Begin Self-Reflecting on
        Every Area of Our Lives...27

    Key Takeaways...31

Chapter 2: What Is Self-Care?... 33

    Creating a Self-Care Routine That Best Works for You.......................35

The Benefits of Daily Self-Care 37

    Bloom Like a Spring Flower 37

    Improves Your Physical Health 38

    Reduces Stress, Anxiety, and Depression 38

    Restore and Maintain Good Health 39

    Increases Self-Esteem and Self-Confidence 40

Inspiring Daily Self-Care Practices to Adopt 41

    Get Moving: Yoga, Exercise, and Stretching 41

    Practice Earthing 45

    Meditation 46

    A Self-Love Meditation 48

    Watch What You Eat and Drink 49

Key Takeaways 51

Chapter 3: Dealing With the Emotional and Biological Aspect of Midlife 53

Susan's Midlife Story 53

The Healing Challenges of Midlife 55

Biological and Hormonal Changes 58

    The Facts 59

    Perimenopause 60

    Menopause 65

Giving New Definition to Your Understanding of Self-Love 71

More Explanations of Self-Love 74

Key Takeaways 76

Chapter 4: The Basics of Emotional Self-Care 79

Sarah's Story 79

Acceptance Will Set You Free 80

What Is Emotional Self-Care? 82

How Can Emotional Self-Care Improve My Life? 83

Why Do Midlife Women Need Emotional Self-Care? 86

How Do You Deal With Emotional Triggers? 87

The Midlife Crises 89

Embracing the Change and Responding to Insights.........................90

    Symptoms of a Midlife Crises 92

    Problems That Appear for the First Time 94

    Problems of Midlife Black Women 96

Successfully Transition to Menopause 99

Dealing With Negative Emotions at 50..100

Healing Negative Emotions on Your Own...101

Ways to Practice Emotional Self-Care 102

    The Art of Forgiveness 104

Making a Fresh Start at Midlife...106

    Your List of Past Unresolved Issues and Associated Emotions ...106

    Your List of New Resolutions 107

    How Do You Feel About Letting Go of These Past Issues? Why Do You Think That It Is Important?...............................108

Key Takeaways..108

Chapter 5: Understanding Criticism 111

What Is Criticism, and How Can It Affect You?..................................111

    How the Whole Concept of Criticism Affects You 114

The Main Types of Criticism That You Might Face 116

    Destructive Criticism..116

    Constructive Criticism..116

Why This Whole Chapter Is More Important for a Midlife Woman ..123

Key Takeaways..124

Chapter 6: Self-Compassion... 127

Understanding the Concept of Self-Compassion.............................127

Why Are Most People Not More Compassionate to Themselves? ..131

Be On Your Team First..131

How to Turn Things Around When It Matters the Most to Our Morale? 133

Importance and Impact of Self-Compassion 134

How Will Self-Compassion Change My Life? 135

The Components of Self-Compassion..135

The Benefits of Self-Compassion 136

Self-Compassion Versus Self-Indulgence 137

You Do Not Have to Be Self-Indulgent to Be Self-Compassionate..138

Making Self-Compassion a Way of Life 139

Key Takeaways...141

Chapter 7: Understanding The Difference Between Self-Criticism And Self-Reflection........................... 143

Self-Criticism..143

Kicking the Habit of Self-Criticism 145

Self-Reflection..146

The Differentiating Factors Between Self-Reflection and
   Self-Criticism 150

   Understanding the Difference Between Destructive
      and Productive Self-Reflection 150

   Benefits of Self-Reflection Summed Up 150

   How and Why You Should Switch From Self-Criticism to
      Self-Reflection 151

The Impact of Self-Reflection 151

Key Takeaways...153

Chapter 8: Starting Your Self-Love Journey.............................. 155

Taking Your First Steps Toward Self-Love as a Midlife Woman 155

Meet Theresa St. John...156

Theresa's Midlife Transition...157

Commit to the Change You Need in Your Life 160

What Your Midlife Journey Is All About...161

Your 30-Day Miracle 162

Understanding the Power of Self-Development and
   the Mentality Shift 163

   What Does Self-Development Mean for Midlife Women? 163

   The Importance of Self-Development in This Stage of Life........164

Determining Your Passion 165

Key Takeaways...170

Chapter 9: The Three Horsemen of Self-Development 171

Learning All There Is to Know About Self-Esteem 171

What is Self-esteem? 173

Tips to Improve Your Level of Self-esteem.......................................174

What Is Self-Acceptance?...177

   Why Does It Matter? 179

   What Benefits Does It Give You as a Midlife Woman? 180

What is Self-Confidence? 182

   Understanding the Fine Line Between Confidence and Overconfidence...184

Take the Self-Confidence Quiz 185

   Self-Confidence Quiz Assessment...188

   How Is Self-confidence Capable of Giving You a Positive Change in Midlife?..189

Hacks Boost Self-Confidence 190

Key Takeaways...191

Chapter 10: Getting Rid of the Problems One by One 193

Problems That Live Beneath Your Personality 193

   Problems That You Might Be Suppressing 195

Measure Your Personality Problems 196

Isolating the Problems and Solving Them One by One...................199

Key Takeaways...203

Chapter 11: The Importance of Setting Positive Boundaries to Achieve Self-Love 205

The Impact of Positive Boundaries..206

   What Are Boundaries? 206

   How Do They Help You Out? 209

Start Working on These Boundaries to Gain the Upper Hand in Situations..210

Determining Your Limits and Setting Boundaries 212

Key Takeaways 217

Chapter 12: Setting Yourself up to Become the Best Version of You 219

Being Older Does Not Mean That You Are Less Than What You Were 219

Physical Appearance 222

Psychological Changes 223

Career Changes 224

The Age Isn't the Problem: What You Think About The Age Matters The Most 225

Your Attitude Is Everything 226

Dealing With All Outstanding Issues Concerning Midlife Head-On 227

Key Takeaways 231

Conclusion 233

About the Author 237

References 243

Image References 251

INTRODUCTION

The more you praise and celebrate your life, the greater your chances are of living one that is truly meaningful at every age.
–Marcee Martin

Life begins the moment you decide to make it count. Like many other women who've reached midlife, I realized that life truly becomes magical when you decide to put the power back into your own hands, to reclaim your natural birthright: real happiness, emotional balance, and authentic creative expression. This is what sets the soul free. When you decide to embark on this magnificent quest to rediscover yourself you can liberate your mind from years of negativity.

I have discovered that this power of choice must be followed by conscious daily action: To care for, and love ourselves in a manner that is compassionate, and empowering. My journey since my early teen years was defined by a seemingly endless series of emotional struggles. I went from being trapped in these emotional whirlpools to totally liberating myself in my midlife years through a series of healing practices that have improved my awareness of who I am now, and why I felt stuck in the past.

My earlier years as a young adult were filled with intense psychological and emotional struggles. I suffered from low self-esteem, chronic anxiety, lack of self-confidence, and a plethora of other emotional disorders. These emotional and psychological challenges impacted me negatively in every area of my life. As I lovingly reflect on those earlier years, I find myself constantly nurturing my journey, now more than ever before. Arriving at midlife was one of the best adventures I have had to date. That's because I decided to begin earnestly reversing the psychological pain that defined my earlier years.

Those constant feelings of negativity that plagued my daily life carried with them a toxic energy that I was not aware of at the time. Every thought has energy too and becomes a vibration that we emit to the Universe. They stay with us as long as we believe in them. Sadly, there are so many women today who are still suffering from similar challenges, and psychological issues, given all the demands that life throws at us. Just like I did in the past, you may also carry a toxic energy that consistently drains you psychologically, emotionally, and mentally.

When you live your life this way, by consistently giving yourself negative feedback, you are bound to also become less productive, and less purposeful, regardless of your age. However, it is not difficult to shift this mindset to one that is more positive, self-compassionate, and uplifting. Age is only a number. It is truly all in the mind and attitude. Your level of acceptance of the aging process and ability to pursue your life's goals purposefully, determines amongst other things, how you approach reaching midlife.

The Best Time for Self-Renewal Is Midlife

It is one of the best times to begin this wonderful journey of self-renewal. Midlife is the period between younger and older adulthood and is accepted as a period of great transition in a woman's life. This transition occurs usually between 35 and 65 years of age. It is a remarkable phase for every woman who is willing to embrace herself fully. At this critical transition, you are most likely bursting with wisdom, experience, and knowledge that you did not possess when you were younger, if only you will give yourself permission to reflect authentically, heal, and expand your awareness.

Reaching midlife can be a lot to deal with if you are not prepared for it, or if you harbor an uninspired perspective about aging. At the core of the new approach required of you at midlife, is your willingness to learn more about practicing *Self-Love*. This entire workbook is aimed at getting you to a place of self-love; to heal from the past and approach this new and important transition lovingly. You will learn more about self-love in Chapter 1, and how to implement it purposefully in your life.

Self-Love: The Best Form of Healing

As I reflect on my own transition to midlife, I stand in awe at the transformation that has occurred in my life after committing to healing with self-love. However, I am aware of how difficult this transition can be for most of us. I can see my younger self pacing my room, racked with self-doubt, low energy, negativity, and feelings of inadequacy. I dreaded social gatherings back then. Every party and office meeting brought out my inner demons. I was too afraid to vocalize my own ideas and I hated the sound of my own voice. I also managed to say all the wrong things. Low self-confidence and self-esteem often bring out the worst in us!

Thankfully I took full control of my life before unraveling completely. In my quest to overcome these shortcomings, I embarked on an inspiring mission. Reading over 200 books (across several niches) in the first year, watching more than 200 videos, and attending many seminars and classes became a new obsession, the purpose being personal transformation from within. That is what I was determined to achieve. In the process, I've acquired a wealth of knowledge in human behavior and created this inspiring series for midlife women, with a great deal of sensitivity about where you are in your journey.

I know firsthand how challenging this transition can be for women. However, I also know how important it is to begin the healing process at this critical juncture in your womanhood. This is the first book of my series for midlife women. It is aimed at guiding you gently toward personal liberation and real success, one that defines who you really are and does justice to your true potential. It is time to start letting go of the negativity that has held you back from achieving real freedom and success in the past. It's not going to be easy, but it will be worth it!

Embrace the Magic in Every Step

Letting go is a process, and healing is an ongoing journey of self-reflection and transformation. It requires your ongoing commitment. You might not get everything in your first read or attempt when implementing the changes suggested in this book. Don't give up. Every little step in the right direction is magical. Soon all those steps will add up.

Creating change is a journey in itself, and the journey is the destination. It is about who you are becoming in the process of creating change. Determination is important, so keep moving forward and stay on the path of creating the change that is required in your life. It will be worth it, I promise you. The mindset shift will occur. Believe in the magic of small steps, and regard each day as a precious new opportunity to change your game.

As you increase your awareness of what requires a change in your life, you will start feeling more inspired, hopeful, and enthused about new possibilities. If you stick with this journey and keep putting yourself first every day, it will just "click" for you, as it did for me. As the title of this book suggests, you will start appreciating how to implement *Self-Love* into every area of your life. It is the driving force for creating positive change.

Let's Aim to Beat the Negative Factors Associated With Midlife

Depression, stress, and anxiety are usually associated with reaching midlife, especially when we are not emotionally or psychologically prepared for it. This first book will therefore help you to prepare your mind to overcome these limitations in your thinking patterns. The aim is to assist you to be more accepting of being older, and wiser, and to show you how to be more nurturing of your inner and outer life.

The chances of enjoying life more now are greater! I think we can relax more and not take life so seriously. That means we can start enjoying life in a mature, inspiring new way, unashamedly on our terms. That is the liberation and success I am referring to, and what you will gain when you start to let go of the past and your present worries. The entire series is dedicated to helping embrace a new mindset about midlife. There is no doubt that midlife women have the potential of enjoying greater freedom in their lives than they ever did when they were younger.

If you are stuck and negatively contemplating the life behind you, then it is time to get unstuck and push the right buttons to reset your mind frame. In this book, I will take you on an inspiring journey of self-discovery in a manner that is nurturing and supportive. Together we will start contemplating midlife not as a crisis but as a blessing. It is a time in your life when you can get really comfortable in your own skin, and release the negativity that no longer belongs to you.

There are many benefits to reaching midlife, and you will discover all of them as you read on. Together we will flip the negative story of aging and being a midlife woman, to a more empowering version of why it is the most important transition that you can make in your life. If you follow through and implement the changes recommended in this book for a minimum of 30 days, and after that at least 10,000 more times, the results will astound you. That is guaranteed!

My Objective Is to Help You Heal

For the last five years, my quest has been to help others just like you and me who have struggled to be truly happy for most parts of our life. This is the first book of my inspiring book series for midlife women. The contents of this book and the other two in the series are designed with care, to help you cope better with this important transition. Do take your time to go through each chapter and work through the practical exercises set out thoughtfully in your self-love workbook. This is your journal to keep for life, cherish, and monitor your ongoing progress. When you look back on your transformation you will feel thankful for what you've achieved.

Reflect on the feedback you will be giving yourself throughout these exercises, and keep writing in your self-love workbook. As you do the work, shifts in mindset will occur. Self-reflection is a powerful way of assessing our thoughts, feelings, and emotions and increasing mindfulness. Awareness is key to creating and manifesting change in your life. You will learn more about improving your level of awareness or mindfulness throughout this book.

If you would love to share details about your midlife struggles, then please feel free to contact me via email at this address: hello@marceemartin.com. I would love to hear from you about how this book has added value to your midlife journey. It would be wonderful to connect.

Summary of Chapters

Chapter 1: Get ready to embrace a brand new understanding of the power of self-love. It is time to heal, and nurture yourself, by attending to your own needs and in this Chapter, I will show how to begin adopting a self-love approach to your transition to midlife.

Chapter 2: Discover the magic of a self-care routine and learn how to apply it regularly in your life, to uplift you and reduce the side effects of stress, mood swings, and hormonal changes.

Chapter 3: Midlife crisis or midlife blessing? In this chapter, you will learn everything you need to know about perimenopause, menopause, and what to do about the side effects.

Chapter 4: Taking full control of your emotions is crucial to staying cool, reflective, and psychologically healthy. You will learn how to achieve this.

Chapter 5: Destructive criticism can destroy a person's soul if left unchecked. Knowing the difference between constructive and destructive criticism is helpful to eliminate stress, depression, anxiety, and negative self-talk.

Chapter 6: Get excited about self-compassion! Remember how I spoke about flipping the switch from negative to positive? In this Chapter, I will show you how to do it!

Chapter 7: There's also a difference between self-criticism and self-reflection. It is important to understand how the latter aims at improving your choices, through the practice of being more mindful as opposed to being critical.

Chapter 8: Turning your life around at midlife is easier than you thought. Learn how Theresa St. John used her mistakes from the past to make powerful new choices when she turned 50.

Chapter 9: Self-love fuels self-esteem, self-acceptance, and self-confidence. It's time to level up your game.

Chapter 10: The magic formula that you need at midlife to transform your life is right here in this chapter. Get rid of your problems and eliminate toxicity once and for all. It is possible with some effort to live without problems, only challenges are acceptable as all challenges have solutions plus we grow from challenges. Problems take up too much unnecessary time worrying about them.

Chapter 11: Most people fear that boundaries may destroy the quality of their relationships with others. On the contrary, healthy boundaries lead to more successful and rewarding relationships.

Chapter 12: Age isn't the problem. Only your perception of aging can be limiting. Learn how to be the best version of yourself every day.

CHAPTER 1

UNDERSTANDING THE TRUE POWER OF SELF-LOVE

If you carry joy in your heart, you can heal every moment. –Carlos Santana

What Is Self-Love?

Before I dive fully into my explanation of what self-love is all about, here's your first journaling task.

1. **Write down what self-love means to you:** Don't overthink it, feel free to write whatever comes up for you. Be authentic. Explore fully your current understanding of self-love by providing your answers below:

_____

_____

_____

_____

2. **Quick Meditation:** Close your eyes and take a few minutes to clear your mind of all thoughts. When you are calm, and feeling centered ask yourself: *How does self-love show up in your life*? Now write down what thoughts have come to you!

_____

_____

_____

_____

_____

_____

_____

_____

_____

_____

_____

_____

_____

_____

_____

_____

It Is Time to Love Yourself

It will bring out the best in you. Not surprisingly, loving yourself will also bring out the best in others. Feeling deserving of self-love will also open your heart more, allowing love to flow naturally to others. When we love ourselves we can also forgive ourselves more easily. This is an important part of your healing journey. There is nothing narcissistic about feeling love for yourself. It is not selfish to love yourself, nor is it an unrealistic goal without relevance.

The trouble is that we've grown more accustomed to disliking ourselves and loving others first, putting others first, and doing our best to please others first before attending to our own needs. Practicing self-love is a powerful way of transforming your life from the inside out. It is not just about indulging in the things you love doing from time to time, like eating dark chocolate, for example.

It is more about honoring your needs first and being more compassionate towards yourself daily. Life can easily chip away at your self-esteem, especially when you entertain negative thoughts about yourself, as opposed to more loving ones. Loving yourself might seem a bit absurd at first, especially if you spent your whole life indulging in self-hate, rather than in self-love.

Self-Love Versus Self-Hate

Most of us are more inclined to love others before we love ourselves. We also have a tendency to come down hard on ourselves. To make matters worse, if you've been subject to severe criticism or have internalized unfair remarks about yourself and you accepted them as truth, then you've been wounded emotionally. This may have created an internal block that is preventing you from loving yourself.

Sometimes we are the cause of our self-hate. Blaming ourselves for everything that goes wrong in our lives, is one example of how we can be unreasonable and insensitive to our own true needs. The better option is to practice believing in yourself more and being open to learning from the experience instead of blaming yourself. Incessant negative feedback is damaging to your self-confidence. Removing yourself as the cause of such unnecessary abuse can be your first act of self-love.

Self-love is transformative when practiced daily. It is about putting your needs first. It does not mean that you become selfish in the process. It is simply an act of being more present and attentive to your own well-being and happiness. You can go from being completely depressed to being more hopeful when you decide to flip the switch from negative to positive, from despising yourself to nurturing yourself more.

Flipping that switch from being negative to positive is an act of self-love. All it takes to achieve this is for you to become more conscious of how you think, feel, and communicate with yourself, and then tweak your thoughts to support your psychological and emotional health. Keep this in mind: Just as it is easy to come up with negative thoughts about yourself, it is also easy to think more positive thoughts about yourself.

Monitoring Your Negative Thoughts

Make a list of all your negative thoughts about yourself: This is important because awareness is key to creating change in your life. Once you've made your list, change each negative thought into more nurturing and positive thoughts about yourself.

For example, *I hate my body*, can be changed to, *I love and appreciate my body for serving me faithfully during all these wonderful years. I choose to nurture my body instead of being so critical, and I choose to make healthier choices each and every day to bring good health and wellness to myself.*

Alison's Lesson in Self-Love

Alison Jacobson realized when she was close to turning 50, that it was time to be more loving toward herself. For the longest time of her life, she was convinced that she was not good enough for anything. At work, she reinforced her belief that she wasn't smart enough when she didn't get the promotion she wanted. She was certain that she was deeply flawed. When her first son died from infant death syndrome and her second was diagnosed with disabilities, Alison blamed herself completely. She did not once consider that it may have nothing to do with anything that she did or did not do during her pregnancies.

Alison was a pro at criticizing herself and blaming herself for everything. Somehow she also managed to play down her successes. "It wasn't the wins I focussed on, it was most certainly the screw-ups," (Jacobson, 2021, para 2). Of course, she also hated her looks. Her physical appearance was disappointing to her. She felt that her nose was too big, and her boobs were too small. When she looked at her eyes all she saw were those sagging bags underneath them. Self-hate was second nature for Alison. She lost her way and hit rock bottom two years before she turned 50.

Alison recalled how on top of her game she was in her twenties. She dated cute guys and had her own business. She also socialized often with great friends. However, it all seemed like a long time ago now at 50. She felt nothing like her former younger self. There is something worth examining when losing your way. You can decide to find your new path back to purpose, passion, and personal power, and totally transform your life from the inside out. For Alison, hitting rock bottom led her to a new path of self-discovery and self-love.

Admittedly, reaching midlife was a huge transition for Alison to make, as it is for most women. Alison got divorced at 40, then remarried very quickly thereafter. Sadly, a mere four weeks after the wedding the man she married was diagnosed with Primary Progressive Multiple Sclerosis, a disorder of the central nervous system. In her own words, she was "stripped to the core emotionally and financially," (Jacobson, 2021, para 6).

Choosing Self-Love Is the Happy Ending You Need

There was a happy ending for Alison. She decided to start practicing self-love, being kinder, more nurturing, and compassionate to herself. She simply decided for herself that it was time to let go of the incessant negative feedback that she was guilty of giving herself when things went wrong. Alison wanted to love herself again, and she went ahead and implemented some inspiring changes in her life. Just before Alison reached 50, she was already experiencing more peace and happiness.

Her new journey started with journaling—expressing her fears, insecurities, and self-doubts—to herself, her new best friend. By doing this she started liberating herself from the clutches of those inner demons and she also started questioning the truth about those insecurities. When she read over her journal entries about her insecurities and became the observer, she discovered that those insecurities were unjustified.

Her next step was to create an action plan which was needed to improve how she felt about herself. This action plan was her act of self-love. It aimed at flipping that switch from being negative and self-loathing to being more compassionate and loving towards herself. She also started compiling lists of moments she felt proud of herself. Soon that list began to grow much longer than her insecurities list.

Alison also started meditating and praying regularly, It became part of her daily self-care routine. These two self-care practices brought her great inner peace and relief from the psychological and emotional trauma of the past. Alison finally stopped being afraid of who she really was. Today she sees herself as a kind, beautiful and intelligent woman. Acts of self-love continue to heal Alison, and it also empowers her to be herself, unafraid of pleasing anyone because she does not feel inadequate anymore. She trusts her intuition and makes bold decisions to preserve her inner peace and happiness (Jacobson, 2021)

Discover Your Real Feelings

Take a few minutes to explore your true feelings about things going on in your life. Now write down the top feelings that come up for you and ask yourself what is the cause of those feelings. Include both positive and negative feelings. For example, is there a certain degree of anxiety that you are currently experiencing, then examine closely what brings on these moments of anxiety?

_____

_____

_____

_____

_____

_____

_____

Ask yourself what you can do every day to start eliminating these moments of anxiety or reducing your anxious reaction to situations. Finding comfortable resolutions that feel right from within is an act of self-love. Then commit to those resolutions.

The Importance of Self-Love for Midlife Women

When you reach midlife, you will go through some major changes, biological and psychological. These changes include how you feel about the life that you've lived so far. As you may have noted with my story and Alison's, there are similarities. Midlife is a big wake-up call. There are many other women who felt this shift took place from within. If you're stuck in toxic habits and activities that are not fulfilling, you are bound to feel restless, depressed, and fed up. Add the hormonal changes to the list, and you have all the symptoms for either a breakdown or a breakthrough! Something must change.

On the other hand, you may have experienced a great amount of freedom and fulfillment in your earlier years, and now in midlife, you are feeling lethargic, and no longer passionate about your current or earlier pursuits. Reaching midlife does sting. It is an adjustment and change is inevitable. It is therefore up to you to decide which way your life will go from here on.

The challenges that women face during midlife are very diverse. According to the Seattle Midlife Women's Health Study in which 81 women participated, midlife challenges for them included changing family relationships, finding a healthy work-life balance, rediscovering themselves, securing financial resources, and coping with multiple stressors at the same time. Some of the other challenges included divorce, break-ups, health problems, and the death of parents (Thomas et al., 2018).

There are some important questions you must ask yourself as you heal and let go of the past, to transition to midlife. It is wise to examine anything that brings you emotional discomfort during this time. This is how you will get to the root cause of the discomfort, to dissolve those past issues. A smart way of handling this emotional time in your life is to do your best to avoid a build-up of toxicity. This is why it is important to create and implement a daily self-care practice. You will discover more about self-care in Chapter 2.

How to Deal With Moments of Regret

If you do experience moments of deep regret, don't beat yourself up over it. At any age, we have some regrets about life. Simply acknowledge them and aim to heal those regrets by taking positive action, that will not lead to a repeat of what made you unhappy in the past. Also, looking for hidden blessings in all situations is another way of overcoming regret and practicing self-love! Self-forgiveness is an important neutralizer of strong emotions, and exercising more of it, is also an act of self-love. Keep this in mind: For every challenge that came your way, there were always hidden blessings that you may have overlooked.

Discovering those hidden blessings in your life will also set you free from trapped unresolved emotions. You have within you the ability to heal yourself. As long as there are rays of hope in your heart, you can heal yourself and make it through this transition feeling great about who you really are! Deep down you are still that person who believes in herself. Healing is a journey of releasing those layers that block out the light of self-love, self-belief, and authentic wisdom. You have all the answers within you already. They are just waiting to be discovered.

Part of your healing journey should always be to find those hidden blessings in challenging situations and to recognize that all lessons were opportunities for growth. This too is an act of self-love. Shed some tears in the process of self-reflective healing, and let it be tears of compassion, love, and acceptance of the beautiful soul that you've always been, regardless of what you may have done or not done in the past. Your life with all its ups and downs was a life well-lived.

Remember that even in the darkness, you can discover your greatest strengths to help you move forward. I am here with you because I know how important it is at this critical juncture to finally be able to heal and let go of years of stored toxicity and self-doubt. Just like Alison, I have discovered the deep wisdom of applying self-love techniques in my own life to ensure that I am living a life congruent with my highest potential and greatest vision.

You Can Change Anything in Your Life

You did your best every time, and with hindsight, you can change anything in your life now. This is why you are here on this journey with me, to heal and move away from self-destructive thoughts that will keep you stuck in the past.

Make this your motto:

> There is no place for regrets in my life, just gratitude, wisdom, healing, and love. Everything that has happened in the past does not make me less lovable. It makes me wiser, and more open to experiencing life on new terms now, my midlife terms. I appreciate how far I have traveled regardless of the setbacks.

When you approach midlife with the above attitude and motto, you can begin to heal authentically and examine your past motivations, and lessons learned with a clearer perspective. You can make new rules and terms for the life that you wish to live now. Midlife is a time of spiritual rebirth, and therefore renewal. It is time to replenish your energy, fill your tank with self-love, acceptance, and inspiration, and take stock of the "something new" you will be creating in your life. Pull out the stops and work on yourself with love as you progress through your midlife years.

Start a Healing Journal

Journaling will help you to get to grips with your transition to midlife. When you journal your thoughts and feelings, they won't feel all jumbled up inside of you anymore. Journaling will help you to organize your thoughts, feelings, expectations, and true goals in life. It will also help you to relook at your old limiting beliefs objectively, to assess where change must occur to flip the switch from being negative, pessimistic, and unmotivated to being more optimistic, and inspired from within.

Start a healing journal today. You can do so on your laptop in a word document where you can type out your feelings every day and assess your ongoing progress. Journaling more regularly will help you to logically work out your feelings. It really does help. In this way, you will also be able to express yourself better. Journaling will improve your level of understanding of what is going on inside you.

You can create many sections in your journal to separate the issues you wish to work on so that it is easy to assess. Ideally, you can list seven areas in your life, and start working on each area separately, to achieve clarity on your healing goals: Vocational, Educational, Family, Love, Relationships, Spiritual, and Financial. It is also advisable to create a section titled; *My Gratitude Journal.* Here start journaling three things in your life that you are grateful for every day.

The idea behind a gratitude journal is to open your heart and mind to appreciate what you have now and to discover the things that are already working for you. Sometimes the things that are not working do tend to overshadow other things in your life that are not working out. Even the small things matter, so don't overlook the little miracles that are constantly in motion in your life. The more often you practice gratitude the better you will feel about yourself and the less negativity you will feel about your life. When you develop an attitude of gratitude you will start noticing the good more than the bad, and this means your entire perspective will shift. Gratitude changes the way you see the world. It is also important to get into the habit of practicing self-gratitude. Say out loud daily what you love about yourself, and are thankful for. It can be anything that stands out for you, like your skills and talent or the way you tend to forgive people easily.

Self-gratitude is a self-affirmation practice that will strengthen your belief in yourself, and get you to see how you sparkle more than you give yourself credit for. You can go deep with self-gratitude, and examine closely how you've pulled through so many times in the past through many tough times. Also, it will remind you that you can get through anything in life if you are determined enough! Determination is a sign that you do believe in yourself, and that is one of the greatest acts of self-love.

Start Practicing Gratitude Right Now! Make a list right here of everything that you are grateful for now in your life. These are the things that are working! Don't forget to mention the small things too. These are the little miracles that make you smile every day!

Explore Yourself More: Let's Begin Self-Reflecting on Every Area of Our Lives

Start by exploring what you've achieved or experienced in the past in all areas of life: Vocational, Educational, Family, Love, Relationships, Spiritual, and Financial. The next step is to read through the contents of your journal and reflect on each area of your life.

Ask yourself: "How do I feel about my experiences and accomplishments, and what creates emotional discomfort for me upon reflection?" Write down your answer to the above question for each area of your life. Offer a detailed explanation of your feelings.

Consider what would make your life more fulfilling today at midlife and write them down.

List your values now at midlife for each of these areas and reflect on how your values have shifted over the decades.

Key Takeaways

- There is nothing narcissistic about feeling love for yourself or expressing love for yourself.
- Practicing self-love is a powerful way of transforming your life.
- Honoring your needs first and being more compassionate towards yourself daily is an act of self-love.
- When you blame yourself for everything that is going wrong, you are being unreasonable and insensitive to your own true needs.
- Practice believing in yourself more and be open to learning from past experiences instead of blaming yourself.
- Incessant negative feedback is damaging to your self-confidence.
- Become more conscious of how you think, feel, and communicate with yourself. Switch your thoughts from negative to being more supportive of yourself.
- Self-care is an act of self-love and when you practice it daily, it will immediately reduce the chances of a toxic build-up.
- Self-care also allows us to reconnect to our spiritual life, and heal ourselves from the toxicity we're still carrying with us from the past.

In the next chapter, we will discuss the importance of self-care. Discover how important self-care is for midlife women, as it will alleviate the negative effects that hormonal changes will have on your body.

CHAPTER 2

WHAT IS SELF-CARE?

The secret of being happy is accepting where you are in life and making the most of each day.

Self-care has ancient origins. Kings and Queens and even ordinary people during ancient times benefited from daily self-care practices. It reduces stress, removes anxiety from our lives, and brings about an inner balance that is vital for our physical and emotional health. Self-care practices help us to feel good about ourselves. It also brings an element of control and comforting familiarity to mundanity. Self-care can be simple or adventurous, depending on how far you are willing to go to completely transform your life!

Self-care can improve how we feel about ourselves, and bring us closer to our inner life. You can also think of it as a daily way of making time for yourself to ensure that you do not neglect any aspect of your emotional, physical, and psychological health. It is a simple way of making every day an extraordinary experience! YES, get excited about self-care as it has the potential to make your midlife journey totally outstanding.

It is a vital part of your healing journey and the greatest act of self-love that you can offer yourself daily. It includes daily healing practices like meditation, earthing, spending time in nature, yoga, exercise, spending a day at the spa, visiting a friend more often, and following a healthy lifestyle that incorporates a healthy diet and physical activity. You can add just about anything to your daily self-care practice, as long as it has a positive impact on your body, mind, and soul. Your aim should be to follow a more holistic self-care focus at midlife, as this will support the changes that you are undergoing.

Make a quick list of all the things you would love to include in daily self-care practice. Maybe you already know the benefits of yoga, meditation, or exercising more regularly but have not made the time to do these things more often.

1.	
2.	
3.	
4.	
5.	
6.	
7.	
8.	
9.	
10.	
11.	
12.	
13.	
14.	
15.	

Creating a Self-Care Routine That Best Works for You

If you have not been aware of the importance of developing and sustaining a daily self-care routine in the past, below is a list of those benefits. We will go through the benefits and thereafter we will discuss the type of self-care practices that can work best for you. Regardless of the lifestyle you follow, self-care habits do not have to take up too much time. Think of it as a worthwhile long-term investment in your physical, and psychological health.

Say goodbye to stress, migraines, and feeling low during the day. Self-care can eliminate these emotional destabilizers from your life completely, something every midlife woman should want! It will also reduce the negative side effects of perimenopause, and menopause, as you will learn more about in Chapter 3. Creating a self-care routine that works for you is all about filling up your day with inspiring little activities that will keep you energized, healthy, and vibrant throughout the day.

As you learn more about self-care, feel free to start implementing some of these ideas immediately. Choose to engage in self-care activities that you enjoy as your chances of achieving success will be greater. Doing the things you love doing will also reduce the chances of making any excuses to skip them. Keep in mind that self-care is NOT a one size fits all approach! Be creative, and fun when choosing a self-care routine. The more time you invest in caring for yourself, the greater the results that will show up in your life.

Also, be willing to embrace tiny steps in your self-care journey. It would be unreasonable to expect results to manifest overnight once you begin this journey. Consistency is key. Make it your time to just be one with your body, mind, and soul, and embrace each step as an important milestone to a happier you. Observe how you are feeling about yourself in your self-care journey, and jot it down regularly in your healing journal, as Alison did in hers.

Once again regular journaling will help you to reflect on the improvements you will experience in your physical, psychological, and spiritual health. You will also get to know yourself better, and increase your awareness of what is important to you in every area of your life. We are all unique and therefore need specific routines that can fit easily into our lives daily, to ensure consistency and personal enjoyment. Choose what you love best, fit it into your schedule, and go for it!

Ask yourself: What do you need to change in your life to bring you closer to enjoying better health and wellness? The idea is to pinpoint habits that are NOT serving you for your greatest good. Your next task is to start changing those habits by choosing better ones that are more supportive of your physical and psychological health.

The Benefits of Daily Self-Care

Bloom Like a Spring Flower

Midlife is your second Spring and it is time to take control of your life, release negativity, and simply indulge in uplifting activities that will heighten feelings of joy, freedom, and happiness from within. These activities are meant to bring about emotional, physical, and spiritual health. When you are in bloom you will feel inspired, recharged, hopeful, and excited about life again.

Self-care is your daily dose of self-love. When you do the things that you love for yourself your body will start releasing more dopamine into your bloodstream. Dopamine is the happy hormone associated with feeling good from the inside out. Stress hormones, on the other hand, do have a negative impact on our bodies. Indulging in stressful activities like negative self-talk can impact our health negatively, and peace of mind.

The over-exposure to stress hormones like cortisol and adrenaline can lead to the disruption of your body's processes and also many health problems. These include anxiety, depression, heart disease, weight gain, high blood pressure, and even strokes (Mayo Clinic, 2021). It is never too late to change your lifestyle. Your midlife journey as a woman is characterized by major hormonal changes. The last thing that you need is more stress and disruption to your body. Leave the stress hormones behind, and aim for optimal health and wellness.

Improves Your Physical Health

Movement is a healthy way of connecting to our bodies. When you choose to do more of your favorite feel-good exercises daily, you will get your daily dose of dopamine. You can also get some fresh air (if you are exercising outside), which is vital for feeling good and releasing stress. Midlife can be stressful but so were the twenties! Each age comes with its own challenges. Just have fun and get physical again.

Also, do pay more attention to your body's nutritional requirements. Hormonal changes at midlife come with special nutritional requirements. The one thing you may not want to take for granted is your metabolism in your midlife years. Now is always a good time to mend your relationship with your body. Practice self-love by giving your body the movement that it needs daily, and the nutrition it craves.

Reduces Stress, Anxiety, and Depression

Incorporating daily simple practices like yoga, meditation, walking in nature, or practicing mindfulness will bring to life a calmer, more poised, and happier you. These ancient healing practices will allow you to relax more, and let go of past unhappiness and those daily little irritants that can build up, leading to burn-out, anxiety, and depression. According to research conducted by Mental Health America (Wong, 2016):

a) Twelve million women in the US are affected by depression.
b) Depression affects women the most between the ages of 25 and 40.
c) A contributing factor to depression is a lack of self-love.

Meanwhile, women who are middle-aged have been found to be at greater risk of sinking into depression. Midlife depression is usually attributed to hormonal changes occurring during this stage in a woman's life. In Chapter 3 we will go into more detail about these changes and explain how they impact negatively when left unchecked.

Midlife is also a time of loss for women. Most midlife women grieve for many reasons. These may include losses of former friendships, the death of loved ones, childbearing abilities, their sexual appeal, former personal identities that no longer work, and the loss of former lovers, partners, and parents (Drevitch, 2022).

Then there are career changes to consider, and other setbacks which are unique to reaching midlife. This is why self-care is important to reduce the amount of stress you experience daily. Self-care will help you to cope better and feel good about yourself again. Most importantly, it will make you feel more accepting of where you are now in your own personal journey.

Restore and Maintain Good Health

Self-care also includes making simple changes in your life that promote wellness, and physical, as well as psychological, health. When you decide to eat well, adjust your sleeping patterns to get an adequate amount of rest, or take a day off to do some bird watching or relax in the spa, you will be inviting health, vitality, and a good work-life balance into your life. Give yourself permission to skip a day of stress, when things get hectic or challenging and spend that time doing something relaxing instead. Use your imagination and make it a day to remember. You will feel great and in control again.

Increases Self-Esteem and Self-Confidence

When you start focusing on doing the things that make you happy, and that have long-term benefits for mental, emotional, spiritual, and physical health, you are boosting your feel-good senses and therefore will increase your sense of self-worth, self-esteem, and self-confidence. We live in a demanding world so as midlife women, it is vitally important to make that extra effort to reap the amazing personal gains from our self-care practices. (Wong, 2016)

You can create your own self-retreat indulgences right at home, to ensure that you are getting your daily dose of self-love! If we've learned anything at all during the 2020 Coronavirus lockdowns, it was to make do with what we have and enjoy it. So you don't have to break the bank to start a successful and inspiring self-care daily practice. Just use your imagination, and experiment with practices that you enjoy doing and those that can fit naturally into your daily routine.

Remember, always believe in the magic of small steps! They all add up. Now that you understand the benefits of incorporating a self-care routine into your lifestyle, below are some inspirational self-care ideas to get you going. I have picked out the top choices for you, which will bring about great results.

Inspiring Daily Self-Care Practices to Adopt

Get Moving: Yoga, Exercise, and Stretching

Exercising in midlife is not what it was like when you were in your twenties, that's for sure. Midlife women are often hamstrung by a lack of motivation and a busy schedule. You may be juggling many responsibilities all at once, whether you're single or not, a mother or a busy executive. It's even easier to neglect this vital aspect of self-care when we are going through big changes in our life, which is why people call midlife a crisis.

Some women struggle to get out of bed, and the thought of picking themselves up may seem like a big effort. If you are overweight or not, skipping moving your body by exercising, doing some yoga or pilates, walking, stretching or swimming will just make letting go of negativity harder. Moving our bodies releases stress, and increases the flow of oxygen into our bloodstream.

When we exercise, those happy hormones; endorphins, are released into our bloodstream as well. This hormone is responsible for bringing down our stress levels and reducing pain. Exercise also fuels brain functioning and improves memory. Research also shows that people feel less stress during and after exercising, and they also experience a boost in their moods. Doing some form of exercise every day will keep those happy hormones flowing in your bloodstream (Johnson, 2022). In midlife, it is important to get regular exercise as it comes with many physical benefits:

- Reduces health risks
- Protects against chronic diseases
- Lowers blood pressure
- Reduces anxiety and depression

- Improves your sleeping patterns
- Improves your heart health
- Improves flexibility

Download your favorite music and go out for a walk in nature, or a jog. If you prefer swimming or any other type of exercise then ensure that you incorporate this daily in your life. Yoga and stretching are also very beneficial: it improves flexibility and mobility, is relaxing, and will ease tension in your body. Yoga is an ancient healing practice that dates back conturies. It is a meditation that unifies body, mind, and soul, so give it a shot. Don't be surprised if you find yourself doing yoga more often than once a day. Scientific evidence shows that yoga does support stress management, mindfulness, weight loss, and quality sleep (Hopkins Medicine, 2021).

How do you feel about moving your body more often through exercising, yoga, stretching, swimming, or any other kind of physical activity?

_____

_____

_____

_____

_____

_____

_____

_____

What are some of the excuses you keep making to avoid exercising? Imagine how great your day will be if you start with a 5-minute stretch, 5-minute meditation, and 5-minute cardio.

Start by taking small steps forward and then gradually expand on your exercise routine by having an evening workout or an evening yoga stretch. Examine your daily routine and work out a schedule that is easy to fit in to get more exercise into your lifestyle!

Practice Earthing

Mother Earth is a natural healer. Make an effort to spend at least 30 minutes of your time daily in nature. Grounding or earthing is gaining in popularity. It is an effective way of releasing negativity from your body. It requires that you walk around barefoot on the soil or grass to ensure that the earth touches the soles of your feet.

You can also simply lie down in your garden with the soles of your feet placed firmly on the ground to ensure that nature's negative ions are absorbed into your body. These electrons from the earth are believed to do more than just release excess energy from your body. Earthing also reduces inflammation in your body and chronic pain. It is also believed to heal your blood (McAuliffe, 2022).

Overall, being out in nature does improve our state of mind and our energy levels. Do you remember the last time you spent time in nature? It always works to feel calmer, and more relaxed doesn't it? Whether it is at the seaside or in a park, in a forest close by, or even just in your garden you will reap the rewards of spending time in nature daily. Do some stretches while you are out there soaking in the sunshine and fresh air. Another great idea is to spend some time meditating in nature.

Here's a fun coloring activity for you! The earth is beautiful and it is just a shame that we don't spend more time out in nature basking in its beauty and tranquility. Commit to an earth hour at least once a week to really appreciate the power of healing naturally while connecting to your natural habitat.

Meditation

One of the lesser-known effects of hormonal changes during midlife is the desire to be oneself. During midlife, it is our hormones that are telling us to be more ourselves now and to take more time out for ourselves, as the level of estrogen in our bodies declines (Well-balanced Women, 2020). There are lots of changes that take place physically, and psychologically during your midlife years. Meditation will help you to remain clear-headed and conscious of these changes that are taking place, so we don't have to be so hard on ourselves.

By meditating each day, you are committing to a life of having more inner-peace, calm, and joyful reflection. Make sure to schedule some meditation time for yourself daily. Once again, you can do this comfortably in your own home. Choose a comfortable spot, create an altar of candles and gemstones to set the ambiance for your daily meditations, light an incense stick or two and enjoy the break you will be giving yourself from daily stressors that can trigger non-peaceful reactions.

Meditation is a chance to give yourself a break from daily challenges and responsibilities. It is time for you to simply sit back, and focus on your breathing while getting into a state of complete relaxation. Here are some of the types of meditation practices you can include in your self-care practice:

Concentration Meditation

It teaches you how to concentrate by focusing on one object at a time, like a burning candle, a rose, or something else of interest. You can also decide to concentrate on your breath, especially when you are feeling stressed out. Simply exhale the negativity and stress from your body, and mind consciously during the meditation.

Heart-Centered Meditation

This involves focusing on your heart center. Sit comfortably and place your hands on your chest where your heart is situated. It is soothing and comforting. Notice any discomfort or emotional blockages that come up for you when you practice heart-centered meditation. Pay attention to these blockages and commit to releasing emotional pain in your heart daily. Use your powerful breath to exhale the emotional blockages and to also heal the pain consciously by deciding to let it go!

Mindfulness Meditation

This is a great way of identifying negative thoughts running through your mind. When you begin your meditation, pay attention to your thoughts and examine the negative ones that you've been running through your mind. Consciously release these negative thoughts allowing them to drift further away from you. You can also replace them with positive, compassionate, and encouraging thoughts instead, or commit to finding workable resolutions for any challenges that you are facing.

Tai Chi and Qigong

These forms of meditation involve movement that uses physical exercise with deep breathing. The movements are slow and look like a graceful dance instead of an exercise. The benefits are great for reducing stress and improving the flow of your chi- or life force (Helmer, 2021).

Transcendental Meditation

This is a wonderful way of empowering yourself and flipping that internal switch in your brain from negative to positive. Choose positive mantras to uplift yourself daily and repeat them at least

108 times. You can also try out guided meditations available on youtube to practice more compassion, forgiveness, and self-love.

Walking Meditation

This is just a wonderful way for you to step out in nature and feed all of your senses at the same time. Soak up the sunshine, and fresh air. Stretch your arms outwards towards the sky, as you begin your healing, and relaxing walks outside. Use your breath to release negativity as you walk, and tune into the alluring sounds, and scenery of nature (Harvard Health Publishing, 2014).

A Self-Love Meditation

Pause and try out this amazing self-love meditation

The best way to boost your day is to start it with an act of self-love. Meditation is a powerful way to enhance how you feel about yourself. Try this out in the mornings. Wake up earlier than you usually do, even if it is 15 minutes earlier. You might want to also include a 15-minute yoga or stretching session.

Here's how to do it:
1. Find a comfortable spot—whatever spot inspires you.
2. Relax in a comfortable seated position on the floor or on a comfortable couch, where you can cross your legs, with your back comfortably supported.
3. Set your intention, by breathing in deeply and out, placing your hands in a prayer position in front of your heart. You can also place both your hands on your chest, over your heart area.
4. Begin to focus on your breath.

5. Become conscious of any constricting feeling in this area. Consciously invite love, peace, and freedom into your heart space.
6. Now visualize yourself surrounded by a brilliant white light. Feel safe in this light and allow this light to release all negativity from your aura.
7. End the meditation by being thankful for at least three things in your life. You can also visualize the day ahead of you and commit to achieving your day's goals.
8. Repeat the words, "Peace to me, and peace to humanity." (Your Zen Growth, 2022).

Watch What You Eat and Drink

Our bodies need proper nutrition and care at any age. It is important for you to reflect on the food that you eat to ask yourself honest questions about your current lifestyle and diet. Does it support your body to fight disease? Is your lifestyle adding another layer of negativity to your life? Our lifestyle can negatively impact our self-esteem and self-confidence. A poor diet can also make you feel bad about your body, health, and choices.

A shift in diet to support your body, and improve your vibrational frequency (to be more positive), is what you must aim to achieve in your life. A positive midlife vibe includes consciously following a more holistic lifestyle in every way possible. The occasional indulgences are allowed. Make moderation your middle name and go for healthier choices; like more greens, vegetables, nuts, and fruit. A diet that is rich in plant-based food will do more good for your body and your hormones than one that contains too little of it.

Make the transition by implementing some moderate changes in your life. Remember the magic of tiny steps and make allowance for consistency rather than setting unrealistic goals that will frustrate you. Eventually, the changes will stick and they will become your new lifestyle. Be patient, consistent, and nurturing to your body, mind, and soul, when making these important changes.

Make a list of the foods you currently consume that are not good for your health. What can you replace them with that are healthier and will leave you feeling better? Come up with healthy replacements and have some fun changing your diet to improve both your physical and psychological health!

1.	
2.	
3.	
4.	
5.	
6.	
7.	
8.	
9.	
10.	
11.	
12.	
13.	
14.	
15.	

16.	
17.	
18.	
19.	
20.	
21.	

Key Takeaways

- Self-care is an act of self-love.
- Self-care, when implemented daily, helps to release stress, anxiety, and depression.
- Self-care brings about an inner balance that is vital for our physical and emotional health.
- You can think of self-care as a daily way of making time for yourself to ensure that you do not neglect any aspect of your emotional, physical, and psychological health.
- Fill your day with inspiring little activities that will keep you energized, healed, and vibrant.
- A daily dose of self-care includes exercise, meditation, spending time in nature, walking, or doing anything that brings you closer to yourself.
- Uplifting activities that heighten feelings of joy, freedom, and ecstasy, will help you cope better with life's challenges.
- Moving your body releases stress, and increases the flow of oxygen into your bloodstream.
- In midlife, it is important to get regular exercise as it comes with many physical benefits.

In the next chapter, we will deal head-on with the biological and hormonal changes that will occur during the perimenopause and menopause stages of a woman's life. Being healthy, and staying healthy must be your priority.

CHAPTER 3

DEALING WITH THE EMOTIONAL AND BIOLOGICAL ASPECT OF MIDLIFE

The relationship you should nurture the most in midlife, is the one with yourself. –Marcee Martin

Susan's Midlife Story

Susan doesn't like the term, 'midlife crises.' However, she experienced an emotional rollercoaster ride when she reached her midlife years. I couldn't agree more with Susan about disliking the term midlife crises. It really is a blessing once we get through the layers of emotional confusion, bouts of anger, sadness, and initial feelings of disillusionment, as we re-examine our priorities. It is the most natural phase for women to go through when they reach their midlife years. Unavoidable too. Still, the changes can be intense.

Midlife took Susan by surprise despite her being fairly content with her life. During her early midlife years, she says that she started feeling more like Jane Fonda, bouncing around in a fitness video! She was somewhat prepared for midlife, as she knew what to expect with regard to the physical and hormonal changes that would take place. However, she was not prepared for the emotional upheaval.

Like most other women going through midlife, Susan started feeling lost in her own life. Her moods were unpredictable and they seemed beyond her control at times. She went from feeling happiness to experiencing anxiety and anger. To top it off, she was irritated by just about everything. Her emotional roller coaster was made worse by her lack of understanding about why all these changes were happening to her.

Her life was changing and so was her mindset. Later on, she understood that the hormonal changes that she was undergoing also played a major part in her mood swings, and they impacted her way of thinking. Her two sons were in high school when Susan was going through all these changes. She still felt needed but in a lesser way than before. For years Susan was the endless grocery shopper, home chef, and chauffeur. However, she was also juggling a job as a newspaper journalist.

Midlife hit Susan like an unannounced guest arriving with all sorts of surprises. Her response to it was just as disconcerting. She could not digest how the last 15 years had flown by. She realized that the hormonal changes had something to do with what she was experiencing emotionally. During perimenopause (the period leading up to menopause) Susan experienced what is normal for women in this stage of midlife to go through.

The Healing Challenges of Midlife

The brain also starts adjusting accordingly during this period, as it adopts new perceptions and considers new choices. We also behave differently and no longer see ourselves as only nurturers being responsible for everyone else's needs. We experience new emotions too. Unpleasant emotions. These include emotions that we've ignored for years prior to arriving at midlife.

Working through these emotions can be challenging. However, it is imperative that you do so. It is the path of healing that really beckons us during this tumultuous and confusing time in our lives. Your body is speaking to you as are your hormones. It is saying, "let's try living our life on new terms." Some of the other changes that Susan experienced included relooking at her priorities.

She wanted to channel her energies into new interests. So it was confusing, with her emotions swinging like a pendulum at times. However, it was also an exciting time in her life. At first, she was worried about her job prospects. Susan still felt purposeful despite the changes she was undergoing. She needed a paycheck, but she wanted it to be meaningfully earned.

To make matters worse, on the health side, Susan was also dealing with declining mobility. In the spring of 2016, she could barely walk around the block in her neighborhood. She soon found out that she was suffering from hip dysplasia and needed a hip replacement. After obtaining hip surgery, she felt deeply grateful to resume an active lifestyle. She also appreciated her health in a new way and vowed never to take it for granted again.

Marcee A Martin

After this life-changing phase and making it past hip surgery, Susan decided that she wanted to travel more, and in 2017 she visited India, alone. This further encouraged her to do more solo traveling. She still travels with her family every now and then but she appreciates her solo adventures just as much. Midlife ended up being a new adventure for Susan, who loves traveling so much. She made it a new meaningful purpose in her life and today she is known fondly as the *Midlife Globetrotter* (Globetrotter, 2020).

What physical or psychological changes can you identify with in midlife? Take your time to identify all changes taking place in all areas of your life to come up with an insightful and detailed response.

_____

_____

_____

_____

_____

_____

_____

_____

_____

_____

_____

Biological and Hormonal Changes

There are many other women like Susan who've experienced an emotional upheaval during their midlife years. The body and the mind undergo biological and psychological disruption. Unless you better understand the changes occurring within you, getting caught up in that whirlwind of emotion will be overwhelming at times. The manner in which you transition to menopause really does to a large degree depend on your state of mind.

In Chinese culture, the mindset of reaching menopause is regarded in a more positive light than in the West. It is regarded as the second Spring in a woman's life. Menopause is therefore embraced as a positive transition. Women in Chinese culture go through the same symptoms, but they tend to handle it with a lot more ease because of their beliefs and mindset about reaching menopause (Jacobs et. al, 2020).

It is accepted in their culture that women should nurture themselves more than take care of others, as they did during their earlier years. They also believe that a woman reaches true maturity and wisdom in her menopausal years. Chinese culture also emphasizes the need to nurture the body, mind, and soul during this phase. Their diet is more nutritional as they regard food as being medicinal to support their bodies.

This explains why only 10% of women in China complain of experiencing discomfort or negative menopausal symptoms, compared to the West's 75%. Exercising, and following a healthy diet remain key to overcoming the negative symptoms of menopause (Vergowoman, 2019).

The Facts

Menopause is regarded as the most striking biological and hormonal change that women experience in their midlife years. Menopause can occur between the ages of 40 to 58. However, even before menopause, your body will start undergoing changes to prepare for it. So you can expect disruption to occur in your body and mind way before you actually reach menopause.

Being aware of the changes that will take place in the run-up to reaching menopause is just as important as understanding the major shift that occurs during and after menopause. Knowledge is power when you apply it accordingly. There are things that you can do for yourself to lessen the negative side effects. I have already introduced you to the importance of self-care during this period. Believe me when I say that it will play a massive role in reducing those negative side effects.

Your state of mind is also important, that is why in this book I emphasize practicing self-love as a way of healing from the past. The last thing you need is emotional baggage to bring you down during this important transition in your life. It is time to let go of the past on so many levels, to make space for a new, brighter, wiser, and more optimistic you in your midlife years.

The disruption that midlife brings begins for some women at least 8 years before reaching menopause and relates to the hormonal changes that take place. A reduction in the production of the primary sex hormones estrogen and progesterone does impact a woman in various profound ways and leads to many biological and psychological consequences. Let's take a look at the various changes that you can expect to occur in your body in midlife (Cleveland Clinic, 2021).

Perimenopause

This stage can occur as early as the mid-'30s or as late as the mid-'50s. When you reach this stage in your midlife years, your body starts moving toward menopause. Your periods will be less regular, and more unpredictable. For some women, the perimenopause phase can last for only a few months, while for others it can go on for many years. Here are the changes you can expect to experience once you've reached perimenopause:

1. Your fertility rate will decline, even though there is still a chance of falling pregnant.

2. Your ovaries will produce less estrogen, as your body starts preparing for menopause, during which your body will stop releasing eggs. This stage can go on for around 8 to 10 years for some women.

3. Your periods may be irregular or you may skip them altogether. Sometimes the flow of your periods may be heavier or lighter than usual.

4. Hot flashes may be experienced on and off. It is the sudden feeling of heat arising in your body, which can lead to the release of sweat. Hot flashes can be triggered by very hot weather, exercising, caffeine, smoking, and alcohol. Therefore always be careful when exercising, and make sure there's lots of cool air around you.

5. Some women may experience vaginal dryness during sexual intercourse, which could lead to discomfort and pain.

6. Be prepared to experience intense mood swings during this phase. (Cleveland Clinic, 2021)

Ways to Cope With Mood Swings, Fears, and Depression

Now that you know and understand the symptoms of the perimenopause phase, dealing with them should be your next priority. Awareness itself can help you move past these low moments that are mainly inevitable for most midlife women. This is also why it is important to incorporate daily self-care practices into your life.

Include yoga, meditation, walking, swimming, going for a massage, and relaxing in a warm bath in the evenings. Feel free to add any activities that you prefer to keep you feeling calm, centered, and poised. Choose activities that are relaxing and soothing for your body, mind, and soul.

These activities will lower your stress levels and prevent you from feeling irritable, low, and depressed. As long as you are filling your day with inspiring activities, as discussed in Chapter 2, the negative symptoms will lessen, and in some instances may disappear or be hardly noticed anymore. Also, ensure that you are getting a healthy work-life balance (Cleveland Clinic, 2021).

A hand massage to reduce stress and tension

We often neglect the hands that we use so much throughout the day. Hand reflexology is a wonderful act of self-love and a quick way of reducing tension in our lives!

Here's how you can do this:

- Prepare to massage your hands by washing them and moisturizing them lovingly. You can keep a set of wipes at your desk and a bottle of moisturizer preferably for the hands.

- Make sure that you have removed all your hand jewelry.
- Moisturizer ensures a smooth and pleasurable massage. So don't skip washing and moisturizing your hands.
- Once you've prepared your hands, shake out the stress by wiggling your fingers, and loosening your hands. Move your wrists in a circle, flex your fingers, then release them, until you are feeling less tension.
- Start massaging the palms of each hand gently by moving using your thumbs to make circular movements.
- Massage each palm separately. Press down in the center of each palm using slightly more strength, hold, and release.
- Finally, massage each finger using your thumb and forefinger, and loosen up each finger.
- Once you are done, focus on your breath by inhaling deeply and releasing stress in your body.
- You can stand up tall and take in deep breaths and shake out stress in your body.

Ways to Prevent Hot Flashes During the Day and Night

Hot flashes during the day or night can be very disorientating. Approximately 75% of women will experience hot flashes. It is caused by the part of your brain, the hypothalamus that becomes more sensitive to temperature when the levels of estrogen produced by your body start to decline. When your body mistakenly believes that it is getting warm, the hypothalamus releases heat to make your body sweat to cool it down. Also, when estrogen levels decline, your blood vessels swell, and this creates more heat in your body (Jacobs et. al, 2020).

During the day avoid going out or exercising outside in hot weather. Keep yourself cool, and stay hydrated, Ensure that you are staying healthy. At night, hot flashes may interfere with your sleep. Keep your bedroom cool, sleep in loose comfortable clothing, and if the weather is hot outside, keep a fan on. What you should avoid doing is taking sleeping pills. Also, avoid drinking any caffeinated drinks at night or alcohol, or eating spicy foods. Have a refreshing glass of milk before going to bed (Cleveland Clinic, 2021).

Dealing With the Hormonal Changes of Perimenopause

During this stage of transition, your body starts producing fewer hormones, estrogen being the main hormone that helps you to ovulate. This impacts your periods. As mentioned briefly above, your periods may be erratic and can either last longer or shorter than usual. Also bleeding during your menstrual cycles may be lighter or heavier than usual. You may also experience a change in premenstrual syndrome (PMS).

When estrogen begins declining, it also causes an imbalance with another sex hormone called progesterone. This imbalance can have many side effects which you need to be aware of. These include a loss in libido. The unpleasantness of this may impact your sex life and can be a source of great psychological pain. So be aware of this and remember that unless you make it an issue, it does not need to be one. This biological phase in a woman's life is inevitable. You can still enjoy a healthy sex life.

You can find relief once again by implementing a self-care practice as discussed in Chapter 2. If you love Oysters then make it a regular indulgence. Oysters are high in zinc and are known as powerful aphrodisiacs. Oysters have been scientifically found to increase your sex drive (Menopause now,

2011). There are other foods that you can incorporate into your diet during perimenopause to reduce the negative side effects of lower estrogen. If you incorporate more plant estrogen into your diet, it will make a difference. Plant estrogen is well known for reducing hot flashes (Cleveland Clinic, 2021).

Here are foods that contain plant estrogen that you should incorporate into your diet (Shecares, 2020):

• Legumes	Chickpeas, lentils, black-eyed peas, split peas, garbanzo beans, and flaxseeds.
• Fruits	Apples, cherries, papayas, peaches, tomatoes, pomegranates, and plums.
• Vegetables	Eggplants, celery, yams, alfalfa, parsley, carrots, and sprouts.
• Nuts And Seeds	Almonds, walnuts, sunflower seeds, and flaxseeds.
• Grains	Barley, oats, wheat, and brown rice.

Here's another list of foods that you can incorporate into your diet. This is a list of food that contain estrogen-promoting nutrients, namely vitamins and minerals that naturally raise estrogen levels (Shecares, 2020):

• Vitamin C	Oranges, lima beans, kiwis, and cantaloupes.
• B-Complex	Spinach, peppers, cabbage, collards, basil, squash, pumpkins, and kale.
• Carotene	Avocadoes, tuna, legumes, brazil nuts, bananas, oats, and turkey.

•	Zinc	Dark chocolate, oysters, beef, spinach, garlic, pumpkin seeds, shrimp.
•	Vitamin A	Apricots, lettuce, bell peppers, fish, winter squashes, dark leafy greens.
•	Vitamin E	Spinach, avocados, sweet potatoes, and almonds.

Lastly, keep in mind that during the perimenopause phase, you could start gaining weight. This occurs as your metabolism slows down. Don't be surprised to note that you can no longer drink more than one glass of wine and get away with it. Maintaining a healthy diet remains key to weight maintenance. Also, ensure that you are exercising. All the above symptoms of perimenopause should prepare you for what's to come next, Menopause (Cleveland Clinic, 2021).

Menopause

This phase occurs in a woman's life when her periods stop for 12 consecutive months. Hot flashes and night sweats are the two most significant changes that take place. Around 57% of menopausal women experience both symptoms. It usually begins at the age of 45 onwards and in some instances, it may continue right up to the age of 80. There are however other changes that women experience (Menopause Center, n.d.).

1. Hot and cold flashes, anxiety, and brain fog are other common symptoms of menopause.

2. Brain fog refers to a condition during menopause that causes you to forget things, or feel slightly confused at times. Practicing mindfulness meditation can help reduce brain fog. Also, keep your stress levels low, and avoid working long hours without resting in between.

3. Formication (the sensation of insects crawling underneath your skin) can also occur. This is explained in more detail below in the next section.

4. Brittle nails can result from lower levels of estrogen. Take care of your nails, keep them moisturized, and use rubber gloves when using detergents.

5. Itchy eyes may also result from hormonal changes taking place in your body. Rest your eyes, and use eye drops when necessary to reduce the itchiness. Use your glasses more often than usual to avoid straining your eyes.

6. Women have also reported experiencing joint pain, anger, and bloatedness. Activities, like exercising more regularly, stretching, meditation, yoga, and eating healthily, will improve these conditions.

7. Hormonal hair loss or thinning of the hair can occur during menopause. This is due to lower levels of iron, zinc, and vitamin B. Consider taking supplements or HRT if hair loss becomes a serious issue. Also, a change in diet will make a difference.

8. Ringing in your ears also known as Tinnitus can occur. It is not too serious to worry about and results from hormonal changes. Exercising, yoga, and doing activities to relax can reduce this condition.

9. A dry mouth or a burning mouth may result from lower estrogen. This hormone is also responsible for the production of saliva. In some instances, you could also experience dental problems. Simple remedies can resolve some of these issues. Sucking on ice, drinking more water, or chewing gum can bring some relief.

10. Paresthesia may occur as well. This condition includes tingling or numbness in certain parts of your body like your

arms, feet, and legs. Exercising regularly to allow for better blood circulation can reduce this side effect significantly. However, if you experience severe pain, then it would be best to consult with a doctor.

How to Cope With Cold Flashes During Menopause

Cold flashes usually occur unexpectedly. The sensation includes feeling a sudden chill in your body. It usually lasts for only a few minutes. However just as hot flashes can affect your sleep and cause discomfort, so can cold flashes. You've already learned that hot flashes are a negative side effect of a decline in estrogen. Well, cold flashes are also a result of changing hormones.

Hormone replacement therapy (HRT) is often cited as a more long-term way of dealing with menopausal symptoms. The solution focuses on boosting estrogen in your body. There are some side effects of each type of HRT. It is not always necessary to go down this route during menopause. The best advice is to consult an HRT specialist before deciding if this is for you.

A more natural solution would be to change your lifestyle. It may be a great time to start feeling naturally good about yourself from the inside out. Exercise more, follow a healthy diet, and cut down or cut out on alcohol, caffeine, and other unhealthy stimulants. Avoid spicy foods. When you exercise for at least 10 minutes a day, you will notice a reduction in hot and cold flashes. Exercise increases your body's temperature naturally. Drink lots of water, and energize your body with the good stuff, like fresh fruit, and vegetables.

Go for foods that contain plant estrogen, to lessen menopausal symptoms. Use comfortable loose clothing at night and accommodate your body during hot or cold flashes accordingly.

Wear more clothes made from natural fabric, and take care of yourself by being more compassionate, loving, and kind (Live healthily, 2021).

Coping With Mood Swings

If you are unprepared for perimenopause and menopause itself, then the mood swings will take you by surprise. You may not understand that your sudden angry outburst or bouts of depression are also correlated to the hormonal changes taking place. The drop in estrogen is directly related to irritability, fatigue, depression, anxiety, anger, forgetfulness, and lower levels of concentration. To make matters worse, women who have a history of suffering from severe premenstrual syndrome (PMS) or have suffered from episodes of depression in the past are at higher risk of experiencing difficult mood swings during menopause.

If you've had a long history of relationship issues then menopause could also compound these ongoing difficulties. This is why healing is necessary, and you can achieve this in so many ways like following a daily self-care routine that includes activities to calm you. The more relaxed, calm, and in control you are, the greater your chances of finding new solutions to ongoing relationships or other issues. Implement self-love activities to nurture, and inspire you.

Doing the things you love doing will give you a natural boost in self-confidence, and leave you feeling better about menopause. It is an unavoidable and very natural part of life for every woman reaching her midlife years. You must therefore do your best to address unpleasant situations, relationships, or any area of your life that is causing you a great amount of stress during this potentially tumultuous period of change.

This is also why menopause is a period of great re-evaluation and change. Your lifestyle will need adjustments to accommodate the menopausal-associated biological changes. Be aware of the negative side effects of menopause, to ensure that you understand what you may be facing. Depression is not uncommon either. At least 1 in 5 women experience this negative emotional aspect of menopause.

Many women also experience intense anxiety, nervousness, and even panic attacks (Dresden, 2022). Low self-esteem is also another common denominator for midlife women going through menopause. Be mindful of what you may be experiencing, and allow yourself to reflect on your life in the process. Working through the emotions will also help you emerge stronger, wiser, and enlightened.

How do you currently cope with mood swings? Have you noticed a shift in your mood patterns recently? Also, describe in detail the fluctuations in emotions you experience. It is not an uncontrollable situation.

_____

_____

_____

_____

_____

_____

_____

_____

_____

Dealing With Skin Irritations During Menopause

Another weird side effect of falling estrogen levels is "formication." It is the sensation that one has of insects running up and down or crawling under your skin. This causes skin irritation and itching. It is the declining amount of collagen in your body, another consequence of lower levels of estrogen. Collagen is a skin-boosting protein and more of it may be required during menopause to alleviate this problem (Dresden, 2022).

Lower levels of estrogen result in drier, thinner skin. This could also result in skin sensitivity to certain products, like detergents, soaps, and certain lotions. If you're experiencing these sensations, or any other severe skin irritations consult a pharmacist or a dermatologist for the best advice on how to deal with this. Today, collagen supplements are widely available in the market and are easy to consume by dissolving it into a healthy shake or fruit juice.

Giving New Definition to Your Understanding of Self-Love

Introspection is important during your midlife years. The emotional upheaval of reaching perimenopause and menopause can be intense. Therefore, it would be better to adopt a more accepting attitude during this period of change, instead of resisting it. Start by reflecting on your entire journey to date, in a manner that is nurturing, healing, supportive and loving. In this way, you can adopt an attitude of gratitude for all the blessings in your life. Be thankful for past opportunities while opening your heart, and mind to new ones on the way!

In this practical exercise you will personalize what self-love means to you at an individual level, by reflecting on your past choices without judgment. Going through perimenopause and menopause can take a huge toll on your psychological health, and holding onto choices you made in your life in the past that still causes you discomfort will not nourish your soul.

Make a list of all major life-shifting challenges that you've had to face on your own. Next to each challenge, describe what you had to do to overcome them, regardless of whether you think they were the best choices or not.

In hindsight how could you have improved on those choices? Pause to reflect on how those challenges have helped you become a stronger woman today. Write down the hidden blessings of those challenges or the hidden blessings of the lessons you've learned in the process of overcoming those challenges.

Notice how you've unfairly judged yourself in the past or negated yourself unnecessarily in the process of recovering from those challenges. Write it down.

Finally, do a self-forgiveness meditation by placing your hands on your heart and saying to yourself, "Under the circumstances, I made the best choices for myself. Thank you. I forgive you. I love you."

More Explanations of Self-Love

Now that you have created your own personalized approach to loving yourself more, here are some explanations offered by other women about what self-love means to them. You will notice that self-love means different things to different women. For some women, it is about caring more about themselves, and being more sensitive toward their own needs; while for others it may be about adopting a more positive outlook on life.

The common denominator though is self-acceptance, this is what it means to love yourself: Self-love is an act of self-acceptance. The Bustle editorial team asked several women to describe what self-love means to them and how they apply it in their lives. Below are some of those amazing and insightful responses (Lusinkski, 2018).

Carolyn

Carolyn describes self-love as being similar to loving someone else, like a soulmate. She says that loving herself includes feelings of unconditional love, compassion, forgiveness, and admiration. Carolyn's best advice is to start to see yourself as someone who is amazing, and lovable. For her, self-love includes having more loving, compassionate, and forgiving thoughts about herself throughout the day.

Rebecca

Rebecca is a fitness and wellness coach and she believes that adopting a more positive attitude toward oneself, is an act of self-love. For Rebecca self-love also includes accepting herself, with her flaws. She always pursues her dreams lovingly and feels content with who she is. This is what she claims, self-love means to her personally.

Octavia

Octavia is an artist, author, and philanthropist and she says that since her work involves thinking of others more than herself, it can be quite draining. After her last bout of depression, Octavia decided that it was time to look within to make sure that her needs are being met. This is how she loves herself and frees herself from a demanding lifestyle. Self-love has set her free! These days Octavia checks in more with herself, to find out how she's doing. Self-love, therefore, is about having an awareness of one's own needs. (Lusinski, 2018)

Key Takeaways

- Perimenopause and Menopause bring about profound changes in a woman's biological and psychological health.
- Perimenopause occurs as early as the mid-30s or as late as the mid-50s.
- When you reach this stage in your midlife years, your body starts moving toward menopause, displaying similar symptoms and side effects.
- Hot flashes and a change in your periods are the first signs of the perimenopausal stage.
- Lower estrogen levels define both the perimenopausal and menopausal stages in a woman's life.
- Intense and unpredictable mood swings are also negative side effects of both stages.
- Fears, depression, anxiety, and nervousness about aging begin in the perimenopausal phase of a woman's life.
- Self-care practices like yoga, meditation, exercise, and following a healthy diet help to alleviate these symptoms.
- Formication is more common during menopause. It refers to the sensation of insects crawling underneath the skin. Hot and cold flashes, anxiety, and brain fog are other common symptoms.

In the next chapter, we will dive deeper into the importance of achieving emotional care. Once again the quality and depth of your emotional transformation during this juncture depends on how you regard yourself.

CHAPTER 4

THE BASICS OF EMOTIONAL SELF-CARE

Happiness can be found, even in the darkest of times, if you give yourself permission to shine your own light when it matters the most.
–Marcee Martin

Sarah's Story

Sarah was 44 when she came off the contraceptive pill. At the time she and her partner were discussing having children. However, a year later her periods were less frequent. She thought she was too young for perimenopause. When she turned 48, her periods stopped. The hot flashes followed, as well as the intense and sudden mood swings. She had many sleepless nights and experienced an electric shock sensation at times moving through her feet all the way to her hands.

Sarah finally saw a doctor who told her that she was in perimenopause. Sarah felt like she had fallen off a cliff. She wasn't ready for this. She was expecting it, but was in a state of denial when she heard the word perimenopausal. She started grieving soon after, for the children she couldn't have, and for her periods that were no more. Sarah also thought about her mortality more often than usual.

When Sarah turned 50, she started accepting menopause. Initially, she was scared about her future. She didn't know how much of life she had left to live. There was also that urgency at the back of her mind that she had to get things done, as she was getting older. The hot flashes made her feel anxious and worried. As you gathered, it was a process for Sarah to accept menopause. Practicing mindfulness, meditation, and breathing exercises really helped her make some changes in her lifestyle to support that transition. Sarah also exercises more these days. She feels better, lighter, and less fearful.

Acceptance Will Set You Free

Acceptance of these natural stages in your life at menopause, is key to overcoming the associated fears, anxiety, and sadness. It is also key to moving forward with renewed hope and wonder. Menopause was a big transition for Sarah as it is for every other woman who has reached this phase. It requires all of YOU to focus on letting something go that was a big part of your life for many years, your periods.

Menopause can be a very lonely journey unless you get the support that you need from friends, family, and healthcare professionals. Reading this book is also a great choice. If you are alone, you will no longer feel so isolated as you read about the experiences of other women in your shoes. Knowledge about this big shift is empowering, and a great way to understand and make sense of this important transition that you are undergoing.

It will release the heavy load of anxiety, and fear, and lead you into the light of self-love (Live healthily, 2021).

Explore: How much support do you have in your life at the moment from family or friends, and how does that make you feel?

What Is Emotional Self-Care?

Self-love has many ways of bringing you the comfort you need during stressful times. When practiced daily you will have a greater chance of healing from any situation that is causing you pain or discomfort. Applying emotional self-care to address your needs, and reduce stress will help you to reduce the impact of any possible event turning into a nightmare, including menopause!

Emotional self-care is essentially giving yourself the support to overcome the negativity that arises from strong emotions. It is an essential part of understanding where these emotions are coming from, so you may examine their root cause, to heal and eliminate them from your life. Your emotions, good or bad, serve you for your highest growth. You can learn how to transcend the negative ones when you practice emotional self-care. The objective is to bring you back to a state of equilibrium or homeostasis, which is a state of balance within your life. Emotional self-care can neutralize negative emotions, and therefore prevent anxiety, depression, anger, and illnesses associated with them.

Emotional self-care is the practice of taking care of your well-being, emotional health, and inner happiness. Your emotions play a huge part in directing your choices, how you feel about yourself, and the direction your life takes. Emotional self-care, therefore, includes checking in with yourself on a daily basis, to ensure a healthy state of wellness from the inside out. The application of emotional self-care in your life depends on what will work best for you! (Social, 2022)

Here's how you can check in with yourself more regularly and avoid strong emotional reactions:

- During the day, consider how you are feeling, and examine any strong emotions that may have come up for you in the day.
- Take a few moments to focus on your breathing.
- Become the observer of the emotions while mentally scanning your body from the top of your head to the bottom of your feet. This helps to improve awareness and allows you to refocus if needed.
- Pay attention to areas of your body where there is any sensation and simply observe it.
- Consciously start releasing negative thoughts, emotions, and energy from your body, and your mind.
- Remind yourself that you are in control. You can pause to better assess the situation to arrive at resolutions.
- Remember that you don't need to react to every thought and emotion as on average we can have more than 6,000 thoughts in a day.
- Always choose a reaction that is more constructive, and communicate effectively with people in a challenging situation, without diminishing your emotional power.
- Once you feel in control, start focusing on your top priorities for the day and get on with them purposefully.

How Can Emotional Self-Care Improve My Life?

Do you remember the last time you experienced intense emotions as a result of a challenging situation? I am sure you can. As you already know from experience, emotions can unravel us, and create a great deal of unhappiness in our lives, unless we deal with them head-on! Every one of us has experienced the power and hold strong emotions can have on us. So I doubt that you won't agree with me.

You may have also noticed how much better you felt when you addressed your emotions and the cause of them immediately in the appropriate way. That is what emotional self-care is all about. The best part is that you can get really creative with the manner in which you care for yourself emotionally. Not only will you feel better and more in control but you will discover some amazing new tools in the process of applying emotional self-care daily. You can also become your own best friend this way. Emotional self-care is nurturing and empowering. You will reap the benefits of being more in control.

The main point here is this: Your emotions will affect you in various ways unless you address them and reach resolutions within yourself. How you care about yourself will also affect the depth of the emotions you may feel in various situations. Therefore, your approach to emotional self-care must be a daily commitment that you make to yourself, with yourself. It is aimed at improving how you feel about every aspect of your life (Social, 2022).

On average a person can have around 6,200 thoughts per day (Berman, 2020). Anything can trigger negative emotions, including the quality of our thoughts. Some thoughts can drain us completely. The human mind, and imagination can create many negative thoughts based on fear of the unknown, and past experiences. We, therefore, need to take full control of our emotions, and not allow those negative thoughts to dominate our lives. If we react to every single negative thought we have, our lives will be miserable. Emotions are thoughts in motion and can create chaos in our lives when left unchecked.

You must make an effort to flip that switch in your mind from being negative to positive, and train yourself to be more focused, present, and purposeful. Taking control of your thoughts includes taking control of your emotions. Thoughts create feelings, and sometimes very strong emotions that can easily derail your attention from the important tasks at hand. This is what creates unnecessary stress in most of our lives. Eustress on the other hand is when we are excited yet nervous at the same time. It is a "positive stress" that keeps us motivated. Being able to make a distinction between positive and negative vibes is important.

Examine: Do you recall a situation in your life when you regretted an impetuous strong emotional reaction to a challenging situation? How did that make you feel later on, and what were some of the important lessons that you learned from that encounter?

___

___

___

___

___

___

___

___

___

Why Do Midlife Women Need Emotional Self-Care?

If you are already in the throes of midlife, fast heading towards menopause, or already transitioning to menopause, then it would have hit you by now just how important emotional self-care is to a midlife woman. In the previous chapter, we touched on how hormonal changes can impact our moods. Without any warning, you can go from feeling optimistic to depressed, angry, or confused about where your life is heading. Regular emotional self-care will reduce the likelihood of experiencing these negative side effects.

When a woman becomes depressed, despondent, or nostalgic during midlife it is usually made more complex by menopause I adjustments the body is undergoing. So don't rule out the hormonal changes altogether. It may also not be a depression at all, but a sadness caused by the transition itself. Also, depression can affect anyone at any age without warning for various complex reasons (Medline Plus Genetics, 2018). So if your moods are erratic and you are not persistently sad, then it is not necessarily indicative of depression. Fluctuating levels of estrogen as well as the mind adjusting to midlife may be the main cause of your struggle to find emotional equilibrium.

To make matters slightly more complex, there are also those unresolved issues at a subconscious level that impacts how you may be feeling at times. This is why dealing with unresolved issues consciously when you reach midlife, will help you to bring your emotions back into a state of equilibrium. It will also reduce the negative impact of the menopausal or perimenopausal hormonal decline in your body. Experiencing intermittent sadness is an expected part of the ups and downs of transitioning to menopause. You're not the exception.

How Do You Deal With Emotional Triggers?

There are ways to deal with it. Practicing emotional self-care is the solution. For example, if you include mindfulness meditation more frequently, you will soon start transcending those negative cycles and just brush it off as by the way. Mindfulness meditation will also help you to get to the root cause of the underlying issues behind the emotions.

During midlife, women do tend to be more emotional, tearful, regretful, and pensive. Therefore ensuring a daily dose of emotional self-care will do you a lot of good, and it won't make you feel so isolated in your quest to transcend the negative emotions that often accompany midlife. The key to achieving this is practicing mindfulness daily (Upshaw, 2020).

Remember menopause will last for many years. The lower estrogen levels will remain with you, all the way to your 80s in some cases. The smart move is to start implementing self-care activities in your life today. In this way, you can check in with your emotions more often to avoid it all piling up on you.

For example, if you find that your mood shifts suddenly in the course of the day, check in immediately, and ask yourself why this is happening. Getting to the root cause of emotional triggers will help you to address issues directly. It will also put you back in control. Be on top of your game in all areas of your life, and check in regularly.

Self-Inquiry: Do you notice when exactly and under what circumstances you tend to feel more emotionally out of balance? In some instances, avoidance of the triggers of those emotional outbursts may help. In other instances, there may be deeper, underlying issues that require your attention. Only when we find long-term solutions for emotional triggers transcend them.

___

___

___

___

___

___

___

___

___

___

___

___

The Midlife Crises

You should also be aware of the midlife crisis syndrome. I wouldn't rule it out completely. A midlife crisis is usually associated with behavioral changes that a person undergoes when arriving at this juncture. These changes are associated with psychological adjustments taking place within a person when reconciling with the sudden realization you've lived for half a century!

Women do experience a crisis of many sorts during midlife, whether it is psychologically associated with getting older or correlated to transitioning to menopause. You are here because you want to either avoid experiencing a crisis or get over it. The aim is to transition properly and healthily to menopause, a natural phase of growth for women.

When you start seeing menopause this way, the transition can be one of joy, and reflection. Joy also includes experiencing pensive moments in midlife. Do avoid attaching good and bad labels to what will happen to you as you transition to your second Spring. See everything as being on the way, instead of being in the way!

If you wish to cry out from feelings of sheer gratitude or self-compassion as you reflect on your former younger self who tried to make sense of life, opportunities, and challenges, but didn't know any better, then go ahead and cry. It is part of the healing journey and will cleanse you. Crying brings relief, and opens our heart center.

Embracing the Change and Responding to Insights

Also, be aware that any midlife "crisis" you may experience, will also be a passing thing. A crisis is also a blessing as it brings to the awareness insights that will help you to transcend things in your life. A crisis is a sign that growth is taking place, and you are transitioning. What people refer to as a midlife crisis is usually a psychological reaction or adjustment taking place in your life. As mentioned earlier, it is a wake-up call of a kind, and everyone tends to react differently to that wake-up call.

If you want to spontaneously enjoy some of the things you loved doing in your twenties, then go ahead and embrace those moments of nostalgia, and relive some of those moments. Unless you put a nasty label on your behavior there shouldn't be any reason to stop you from reliving any aspect of your past that was fun. In fact, going down memory lane can be very healing, and cathartic, and it does increase feelings of self-love, self-compassion, and appreciation in between some regrets. Since you are the person going through a midlife transition, you will instinctively know what to do to feel better about yourself, and your unique journey. Believe in yourself.

If you loved going on picnics or dancing when you were in your twenties and got so busy over the years that you forgot how good those pleasures made you feel, then who's to say that in your midlife years, you're not allowed to enjoy these things once again? As long as you are aiming for "feeling good" about yourself again there's no harm in that. I doubt very much that we become so unconscious during midlife that we cannot be accountable for our decisions or actions. Some men and women do use midlife crises as an excuse of a kind to get away with being reckless. It doesn't have to be that way for you. If it is a reckless crisis then at a subconscious level, those choices are reflective of unresolved issues. That's all.

My advice to you is to find the middle path that does not jeopardize the things that are dear to you when going through a midlife transition. Do things you love doing to uplift you and not bring you down or lead to more negative consequences in your life. If you foresee careless choices on the way, then seek advice from a counselor or friend. Talk things through before being rash. As a rule of thumb, do avoid following the path of negative self-talk during midlife. Also isolating or hurting yourself in the process of reaching midlife will not benefit you. You don't have to have a crisis when reaching midlife. By practicing self-love you can embrace your midlife years as a blessing, and open a new adventurous chapter in your life.

Ask yourself: What are some of the psychological adjustments you made upon reaching midlife? Were they painful, or fun?

___

Symptoms of a Midlife Crises

The following symptoms of a midlife crisis are applicable to both men and women.

- Feeling unfulfilled.

- Feelings of regret, and nostalgia at the same time about the past.
- Experiencing boredom, emptiness, and lack of purpose.
- Being impulsive and making rash decisions to boost yourself up.
- Sudden dramatic changes in behavior.
- Infidelity or constant thoughts of infidelity.
- Comparing yourself to others, younger persons who appear to be more fulfilled than you. (Upshaw, 2020)

The crisis usually begins with denial and leads to acceptance of reaching midlife. However, getting to a stage of acceptance is a journey that does also require emotional self-care. According to the Merriam-Webster dictionary, a midlife crisis is, "A period of emotional turmoil in middle age characterized especially by a strong desire for change (Mind Tools, n.d)."

That's a great definition and hits the nail right on the head (in other words, it is the most appropriate definition). Midlife is characterized by change, and we all react differently. So don't judge it. Rather embrace it as an awakening and dive deep within yourself for insightful, inspired wisdom. Even amidst the emotional confusion, and chaos, you can achieve clarity in all matters of your life. We can also try replacing the term "midlife crises," with something else that fits how we experience it. The word crises carry a negative connotation to it.

I find the term "midlife transition" to be more apt, and it does have a more positive ring to it. A crisis of any kind always presents us with opportunities for growth, development, as well as new opportunities. Whatever bubbles to the surface for you during this transition, my advice is to embrace it as a hidden blessing and explore what it means to you at a deeper level. Be curious and work your way to feeling enthused about the prospect of the transition. After all, it is unavoidable, so a winning attitude would be in order, don't you think?

Problems That Appear for the First Time

The problems that appear in your life during menopause or even perimenopause in midlife are unlike any other that you've faced as a woman. It's a completely new phase that you're entering. Just like you experienced challenges when you were a teenager transitioning to puberty, you are entering a "new unknown" at midlife. Think of it as a new growth phase in your life. When you were a teenager you also had to go through a transition phase. If you recall, it wasn't always pleasant transitioning to your teenage years and then to becoming a "young adult."

Similarly, in midlife, you can expect new challenges to overcome. Declining estrogen as you have already discovered in Chapter 3 will not be a thing of the past once you reach menopause. It will be an ongoing issue for the rest of your life. Just as you had to accept that your periods will be with you for a very long time when you reached puberty (that was hard for some of us), the opposite is happening now as you journey towards menopause.

Life without your periods is not one that is going to be all doom and gloom. See yourself as a woman who has transcended some of the earlier demands of life. At last, you're in full bloom and you can own your qualities without fear, guilt, or second-guessing yourself. Midlife is a time to experience complete liberation from all the earlier demands that life placed on you. You've earned it, so celebrate it!

It is important to look back on the years you left behind when transitioning to womanhood, and approach your new journey to menopause in the same curious way you did when you were a teenager. The difference now is that you have the wisdom and confidence to take full control of your life and be completely accountable for your happiness. Self-love will show you the way to greater happiness!

Celebrate your achievements: List all the highlights and achievements in your life that really matter to you. Include all the reasons why you feel proud of yourself for being a strong, and successful woman! **Remember that how you measure success is more important than how the world measures success!**

_____

It is time to pay tribute to your past successes and accomplishments. Why not make a date with yourself or friends to share in each other's success stories and celebrate them? Order your favorite dinner if you don't feel like a night out on the town. Just do what matters to you. Go ahead and celebrate your life's achievements in some amazing unique way. You deserve it!

Problems of Midlife Black Women

Approaching midlife in some communities do have their own challenges to contend with. The Washington Post published an interesting article that discussed how black women are impacted by midlife, as they transition to menopause. A two-decade study of women of different races experiencing menopause provided some evidence of these challenges. Some of them are not biological but are more psychological, based on certain beliefs about menopause that some black communities have adopted (Schaaf, 2021).

Menopause appears to be either a taboo topic in some black communities or a difficult topic to get around. It has also been found that there exists some mistrust in black communities about getting medical advice offered by professionals about menopause. However, as an individual, it is your choice to overcome any stigmas associated with menopause in your community. Keep this in mind: Menopause is unavoidable for any woman who reaches midlife, steadily heading towards her golden years.

If you follow all the advice in this book, the benefits will accrue to you, regardless of race, religion, or culture. Perception can be a powerful inhibitor, so do let go of any negative stigma associated with menopause, and embrace self-love instead. It is also important that you overcome the silence about this topic. Menopause is a big deal, and it is what you're heading toward if you haven't reached it yet. Involve your loved ones in your discussions about menopause, and share your concerns with them, to come to mutually acceptable changes you envisage making about your lifestyle. For example, you might be considering a career change. In this case, you will need all the support and encouragement you can get.

Involving your loved ones in your discussions on menopause will bring you closer to them, and will help you to receive the appropriate support that you need. It may very well eliminate your mood swings altogether. A well-managed transition at midlife is the elixir needed to overcome many of the negative side effects. Doctors can play a meaningful role in the lives of women undergoing menopausal or perimenopausal changes. So don't avoid reaching out to a medical professional for advice.

Ask yourself: What are your fears and concerns about menopause? How important is it for you to overcome them?

Successfully Transition to Menopause

Get Comfortable With Menopause

Take charge of this phase of your life and find out all that you can about it. This will help you to make adjustments in your life, regardless of society's perception of menopausal women.

1. **Every Woman Is Unique**

   As you know already, every woman is unique regardless of race, culture, or ethnicity. Therefore menopause will be different for each individual woman. Accept that your journey will be unique and it all depends on how you approach this new growth phase in your life.

2. **Listen to Your Body**

   Our body communicates with us daily. When you eat something that leaves you feeling uncomfortable it is a sign that you should avoid that food. When you are feeling excessively hot or cold, attend to it immediately, by taking action to reduce the discomfort.

3. **Knowledge Is Power**

   Talk to your doctor, and ensure that you get the proper medical support needed to suit your specific needs. We've discussed the hormonal, biological, and psychological impact that menopause may have on you. It does help to reach out to your trusted doctor to expand on your understanding. Make a list of questions and concerns, and get to the bottom of things.

4. **Share Your Experiences**

   Talk to friends, family, your partner, and even other women in support groups if need be. This will also assist you to transition properly, gain more support, and avoid feeling isolated, alone, or depressed. (Jacobs, et. al, 2020)

Dealing With Negative Emotions at 50

Negative emotions always complicate things in life. As we get older and wiser we may improve in some ways when it comes to how we handle negative emotions. However, it is not altogether true that older people can properly contain their negative emotions. As you discovered earlier, when Sarah turned 50 and her periods were suddenly a thing of the past, she had a hard time coping with this shift. So have many other women in midlife facing this transition. By the mid 40s, there are bound to be negative cycles that we start encountering regardless of how brilliantly we may have lived. The transition begins in the mid-40s for most women and can reach a climax between ages 50 and 55, just as Sarah did.

Negative emotions for women in their 50s center around the perception of mortality, and biological changes. This in turn impacts other areas in their lives and can affect their overall self-confidence and self-esteem. Women at 50 also tend to start examining the quality of the life they have lived. This is a great thing, as self-reflection is key to making improvements in the areas of our lives that require change. Emotional self-care will definitely help you to cope with any kind of negative emotions you experience along your midlife journey.

Negative emotions include feelings of anger, regret, shame, sadness, hopelessness, apathy, jealousy, and all other feelings associated with toxicity, and self-hate. I am sure that you may recognize some of these emotions and know how unsettling it is. Even though avoidance may seem like the best option at first, it is not. In fact, it is the worst choice you can make as avoidance does nothing more than delay things for a while. It may be better to vent and get it out of your system as avoiding these negative emotions may build up and create more toxic results in your life (Scott, 2008).

Avoidance or denial are painful ways of dealing with negative emotions. Often it can lead you down the path of addictive or destructive behavior as a way of numbing the impact. There are always more options available to deal with negative emotions. The best choice would be to face them head-on. It will reduce the impact, help you to get to the root cause of the emotions, and it will lead you down the path of healing. This way of dealing with negative emotions is great for all aspects of your wellness; psychological, physical, and spiritual.

Healing Negative Emotions on Your Own

1. **Name It.** If you are experiencing jealousy, anger, hate, or insecurity: Call it out loud and clear. Say to yourself that right now you are feeling this emotion. Naming is a powerful way of accepting what you are feeling. Acceptance leads to inner peace and more positive action.

2. **Describe It.** Describe to yourself what this emotion feels like. Ask yourself how it is making you feel and why it is making you feel that way. Is there a particular cause for anxiety that brought up this emotion? What are your options regarding eliminating these emotions from your life?

3. **Eliminate It.** Your next action should be to take a closer look at all your positive traits. Stack up your best qualities by writing them down in your journal. Expand on each one of your positive traits, and honor it by justifying how it has served you throughout your life. Doing this will uplift you,

and bring into balance the true image of yourself. You may want to include a self-love meditation by focusing on your heart center. Finally, make firm resolutions to move away from the current psychological state you're experiencing. You can make a list of the things that are worth more of your energy, and start releasing the negative experience from your subconscious mind as the dominant thing in your life.

Always count your blessings in moments of weakness. It opens the heart and rebalances your perception of your life. Often when we are negative, our perception of ourselves becomes skewed and blinds us to the things that are worthy of gratitude. So do make an effort and a powerful choice to move further and further away from those negative thoughts, vibes, and actions that can potentially keep you stuck in a seemingly endless cycle of negativity. You will figure things out when you are feeling positive and vibrating that inner youthful light from within (Ready, 2012).

Ways to Practice Emotional Self-Care

1. Self-Acceptance

Know thyself, be thyself, and heal thyself! When you accept yourself, love yourself, and stop pushing yourself down as a result of unreasonable expectations, you will feel great from the inside out. Just as you would nurture a child, and support your child regardless of their weaknesses, do the same for yourself. Nurture your inner child, accept both your strengths and weaknesses, and aim to improve yourself lovingly in areas of your life that require healing. Compliment yourself and feel good when others appreciate you back (Nollan, 2020).

2. **Practice Mindfulness Meditation**

   Take a few minutes each day to pause and reflect on your emotions. You can achieve this by practicing mindfulness meditation. Create short, five-minute mindfulness exercises during the day to pause, breathe in deeply, and let go of the negative emotions as you notice them. At the same time, you can flip the switch from negative to positive and this will shift your reaction to present and future challenges that may arise.

3. **Talk to Someone or Find a Therapist**

   It helps to talk things through with a friend or two. Start your own circle of midlife women to share your challenges, laugh, and comfort each other. Alternatively, you can also look for a credible therapist in your area. It can be very beneficial for youtube to attend to your mental health challenges by talking to a professional therapist. Talk therapy is a good alternative for releasing negativity and stress in your life. Plus, you will receive the professional support of a therapist that has your best interest at heart (Olivine, 2022).

4. **Do What You Love**

   Add a dose of self-love to your day every day. Choose to do more of the things that bring you joy, and that make you smile. When you do what you love and love what you do your emotional health will improve naturally. Once again, fill your day with meaningful activities. Do work that you enjoy, move your body by engaging in your favorite sport, go for a massage every now and then, and take up a hobby that unleashes your creative side!

Make a quick list: Write down all the things you love doing and what you should be doing more of in midlife.

1.	
2.	
3.	
4.	
5.	
6.	
7.	
8.	
9.	
10.	
11.	
12.	
13.	
14.	
15.	
16.	
17.	
18.	
19.	
20.	

The Art of Forgiveness

The moment you see yourself as being worthy of love, you will also see yourself as being worthy of forgiveness. This is an important step towards dissolving past or present hurtful issues. Love is a powerful healer. Sometimes though, forgiveness is a process. It is part of the letting go process, and it may be necessary to work on specific issues diligently over a period of time to ensure complete closure. Therefore be patient with yourself. It is not necessary to force the process of forgiveness to occur instantaneously. Work through all the complex emotions and turn negatives into positives that work for you.

When we hold on to past hurts, we are constricting the flow of love. Practice the self-love meditation at the end of Chapter 2 every day if you find yourself struggling with forgiving yourself. Unresolved issues are bound to create discomfort. By deliberately focusing on loving yourself more, you will feel worthy of forgiving yourself. Remember that any discomfort you experience in your heart area is an indication that more healing is necessary to dissolve the discomfort.

Keep in mind that some issues may be easier to resolve than others. As long as you know what those issues are, and you are constantly filling your day with inspiring activities, it is only a matter of time before you dissolve those issues, thus achieving a breakthrough. Be patient and persistent, practice self-compassion, and find ways of filling your heart with love, regardless of your ongoing emotional struggles.

Forgiveness is also an act of self-love. Our anger directed at people and events from the past is usually a transferred emotion of anger, disappointment, or shame we feel for ourselves. We beat ourselves up because we are judging ourselves for making mistakes. However, every perceived mistake offers us valuable insight and lessons. These are the hidden blessings from which we grow into wiser individuals. It's never too late to make a change and forgive yourself.

Marcee A Martin | **105**

Making a Fresh Start at Midlife

- Make a list of unresolved issues.
- Next to each unresolved issue, name the emotions that are attached to them. For example anger, jealousy, resentment, etc.
- Write down the reason these emotions have stayed with you for so long.
- For every emotion you've listed is it possible that you've misjudged yourself in the process and you're still angry with YOU?
- It is time to forgive yourself, and honor your unique qualities without making comparisons with anyone else.
- Now ask yourself, how can you ensure that these issues will not recur in your life again? Make new resolutions based on the hidden blessings and the tough lessons.
- Do a self-love meditation as described in Chapter 2, and send love, healing, and forgiveness to yourself. Do this for 30 days without interruptions. Increase your self-love list by spending more time doing the things you love.

Your List of Past Unresolved Issues and Associated Emotions

1.	
2.	
3.	
4.	
5.	
6.	

7.	
8.	
9.	
10.	
11.	
12.	
13.	
14.	
15.	
16.	
17.	
18.	
19.	
20.	
21.	
22.	

Your List of New Resolutions

1.	
2.	
3.	
4.	
5.	
6.	
7.	
8.	
9.	

10.	
11.	
12.	
13.	
14.	
15.	
16.	
17.	
18.	
19.	
20.	
21.	
22.	

How Do You Feel About Letting Go of These Past Issues? Why Do You Think That It Is Important?

Key Takeaways

- Emotional self-care is essentially giving yourself the support that you need to overcome negativity.
- The objective of practicing emotional self-care is to bring you back to a state of equilibrium or homeostasis so you can feel good about yourself, and your life.
- Emotional self-care helps us to make better choices.
- It neutralizes negative emotions and therefore prevents anxiety, depression, anger, and illnesses associated with them.

- Emotional self-care is the practice of taking care of your well-being, emotional health, and inner happiness.
- Check-in with yourself every day to determine the health and wellness of your thoughts, feelings, and emotions.
- You can decide what will work best for you when it comes to your emotional health.
- Make a commitment to improving how you feel about every aspect of your life.
- Anything can trigger negative emotions, including the quality of our thoughts.
- You must make an effort to flip that switch in your mind from negative to positive. Do train yourself to be more focused, present, and purposeful.

In the next chapter, you will learn everything about criticism and how it fits into your life. Knowing and understanding the difference between destructive and constructive criticism is key to your ongoing journey of self-love.

CHAPTER 5

UNDERSTANDING CRITICISM

Criticism can fuel more self-doubt while love on the other hand will give you confidence, and nourish your soul. –Marcee Martin

What Is Criticism, and How Can It Affect You?

I think we all instinctively know the answer to the above question. Our reaction is the most important part of how criticism can affect us. We can choose to react strongly only to later internalize the criticism when on the receiving end, or we can listen objectively and decide for ourselves whether the criticism is justified or not. The latter option is the most powerful way of dealing with criticism. However, that takes a fair amount of emotional intelligence to reach a state of objectivity. Handling criticism isn't all that bad, once we've ingested the self-love bug into our system, we can judge for ourselves, what is fair criticism and what is not. We've earned it as midlifers!

Here's the thing about criticism which you probably already know: There will always be someone who will criticize you, so being able to make that distinction is important. Sometimes we are our harshest critics. We've also experienced failures in life, and you probably know that this can lead to a mountain of self-criticism during those dark spells. Everyone has experienced failure in one way or another because that is another way of learning and growing. However, now you should know better. There is nothing wrong with you for trying and failing, or making mistakes in life. It was Winston Churchhill who wisely said, "success is not final, failure is not fatal. It is the courage to continue that counts." (CNBC, 2020)

Criticism by its very nature is destructive. So yes, when you are on the receiving end and on the giving end, the result will not be positive. There is a difference between criticism and feedback. These are two different concepts altogether. So let's get very clear on this. Feedback is NOT the same thing as criticism unless the objective is to break down a person or destroy their mood as a malicious way of hurting them. Criticism leads to conflict in relationships and within yourself.

Therefore, as a rule, we should avoid internalizing criticism and lashing out at others critically. You will not ever completely meet the standards or expectations of everyone, but you will come close to meeting the expectations of reasonable, empathetic people who are not perfectionists. That is your aim. Dialogue and effective communication in a manner that is more empathetic will lead to the best results. Make that your mantra!

Let's make a list: When and where in your life did you react very strongly to criticism? Take your time to pinpoint moments when you were the most affected by criticism and also when you were least affected.

How the Whole Concept of Criticism Affects You

If I say to you, "Gosh you've gained a lot of weight since reaching menopause, I hardly recognized you. I hope you plan on losing all that weight honey because if you keep it, you'll be mistaken for someone's great grandma!" Ouch, that definitely stings, doesn't it? We've all had some moments in our life when someone's criticism knocked our socks right off. Whether criticism is constructive or destructive, it is bound to sting.

Therefore the idea is to focus on providing positive feedback to yourself to eliminate the sting of criticism from our lives completely. In this way, you will learn to be more compassionate, and empathetic, and you will be in control of your reactions to any type of criticism that is thrown your way. Sure there will be moments when we are bound to be affected. However, we can decide in those moments to be loving and compassionate to ourselves by flipping that switch from negative internal feedback to more positive internal feedback.

Both our reactions to the earlier criticism would most likely be something like, "Oh my God how insulting was that comment about my weight! I must really look old, ugly, and hideous now that I have gained all this weight and reached menopause." However, the best choice would be to switch the negative internal dialogue to positive internal dialogue, "Who cares what she or anyone else thinks of me? So I have gained weight. I've been through a lot lately and it is okay to be human. I know that if I want to lose this weight I can, and it's not so bad being someone's great-grandma. To the devil with such a heartless comment. I am me, and I have been through some changes. It doesn't make me less beautiful or less worthy of love."

This is the way to handle things within ourselves when facing criticism. It is the only way to avoid internalizing the false perceptions that others may have of us. No one is walking in your shoes but you, and therefore you are the best judge of who you are, and what you stand for. You can handle criticism objectively. Yes, you know that you have gained/lost weight. There is no doubt about that. Listening to it as a form of criticism is an unhealthy way of dealing with the observation.

A better way would be for you and ONLY you to decide how you should feel about it. You can choose a positive, more loving response to your weight gain or you could choose a more humorous response. For example, you can joke with yourself privately or with your close friends about how much you've enjoyed eating spicy exotic foods recently to spice things up at menopause, and now that your little love affair with spicy food is over you're thankful for the experience and looking forward to a new adventure of getting back to healthy!

The Main Types of Criticism That You Might Face

Destructive Criticism

The above example was a good one of destructive criticism. I like to think of this type of criticism as a statement that is meant to destroy your soul because this is what it can potentially do to someone, especially a sensitive person. It is therefore not in your best interest to continue to listen to anyone who is offering you destructive criticism. Simply walk away from such a situation. If you're facing off with an angry customer on the other hand or an angry boss, then deal only with the issue at hand professionally and do point out that you can resolve this without personal attacks being made against you.

Constructive Criticism

Construction criticism can also sting a bit. However, if you are a mature, reasonably approachable person, you can learn to appreciate constructive criticism as feedback that is meant for your personal growth. Especially in a professional setting, being blunt with anyone about their work can push a person to strive to be better, and to achieve better results. I still think that offering objective feedback is more constructive than being overly critical to any degree.

Super sensitive persons may also not be agreeable to the blunt approach of constructive criticism even if it's to a large degree honest. Constructive feedback is the best way to show support while pointing out changes that will improve a situation or your or someone else's work. Constructive feedback lets the person know that you do care about their feelings and that you have their best interest at heart.

Making the distinction between constructive and destructive criticism for yourself: Think about times in your life when you were harsh with those you love, and reflect on how you hurt someone else's feelings. Write down those moments that could have been avoided had you been more empathetic and compassionate.

_____

_____

_____

_____

_____

_____

_____

_____

_____

_____

Now that you have completed this exercise, you probably realized even more how important it is for us to reflect on the love and care we deserve to receive from and give to others. We are all worthy of love, compassion, kindness, sensitivity, and empathy. Therefore, let us commit today to be less critical and more caring, effective, and purposeful in our feedback to ourselves and to others. Self-love also includes how we treat others. What we often despise in others we see in ourselves. Those are our rejected qualities. What we love in others we also see those qualities in ourselves, as the more acceptable qualities.

Therefore, treat others in a way that you would love to be treated, by offering feedback and less criticism. Even in the most trying situations, you have the power within you to turn things around. Any situation can end up being more workable with conscious effort. Do avoid judging yourself too harshly too if you experienced outbursts that were hurtful to others. Forgiveness is available as long as you do not give up on yourself, your humanity, and your compassion.

The Characteristics of Destructive Criticism

- It is often a personal attack and can emotionally hurt a person.
- Focuses on blaming someone for a problem and not on solving conflict to ensure that all parties are honored, heard, appreciated, and acknowledged.
- Often leads to negative consequences for both parties or all parties concerned, and may lead to a complete breakdown in personal or professional relationships.
- Creates tension in teams, and often destroys the morale of individuals and teams.
- It can lead to trauma, stress, and long-term depression.
- The intent behind destructive criticism is to undermine hurt and offend.
- It is usually harsh and can also damage someone's reputation professionally or personally.
- It leaves the victim feeling grossly underappreciated for their efforts.

- Destructive criticism can be very subjective and is unrelated. It is a personal attack.
- It is demeaning, insulting, and humiliating.

The Characteristics of Constructive Criticism

- It is often used to solve problems and not create more problems.
- Used to assist others to improve themselves personally or professionally.
- While it may still hurt sensitive people, it can be beneficial for a person's growth.
- When you give constructive criticism you show respect for someone's feelings.
- Constructive feedback may not be personal but mainly serves as feedback.
- Another way of viewing it is referring to it as critical feedback.
- It is more objective and less insulting, demeaning, or soul-destroying.

When you offer constructive criticism you are saying to someone that you value them and would love for them to improve. However, the intention is important, and when it comes to criticism that is personal it can still be unjustified, and not necessary. The focus of constructive criticism is improvement when communicated in that spirit, and that is the best way to determine if someone cares about you or not.

Ultimately you are still the judge and the jury of your own actions. Being more open-minded to constructive criticism can definitely lead to new insights and even new opportunities. So be objective and aim to implement change if necessary to improve, when you know deep down that you could use some help (Paretolabs, 2021).

Answer this insightful question: Do you remember how constructive criticism helped you to improve your skills or behavior in the past?

Why This Whole Chapter Is More Important for a Midlife Woman

As you've probably gathered much earlier in this book, I am writing it because I care and I know what it feels like to spend many years trying to figure things out and get away from negative, that of my own and of others. As if we did not have enough criticism, the last thing we need is more of the same at midlife. Now is the time to change things, shake things up, and absolutely refuse to be despondent, negative, and self-destructive. Your mindset will determine whether you make it or stay stuck in the same old negative vibes and endless cycles of interspersed moments of happiness if you are lucky enough.

Enough of that. You are the only person in the Universe who gets to decide what will affect you psychologically. Sure, you will still have some negative moments every now and then. However, it doesn't have to last for more than a minute if you can help it. Spicing things up in your life does not have to include jetting off to some far-away exotic island to forget your issues for a while. When you return from your luxurious holiday, your issues will return with you, unless you face them, heal them, and simply refuse to be affected by anyone's unjustified criticism of you.

Midlife does not need to be a soul-destroying journey. It is going to be the best years of your life because you are now done with all the bullshit. It is totally your call now. You can decide if you want more self-criticism or more self-love. I bet you already know the answer to that and I am proud of you. Choose not to criticize those hot flashes, irregular periods, or mood swings. Simply choose to experience the ups and downs knowing that you are fully prepared for them, and have with you new tools to get through things. There is nothing more empowering than a woman who knows who she is, and what she is capable of. You are that woman now.

Key Takeaways

- We can choose to react strongly to criticism when on the receiving end, or we can listen objectively.
- You are the ultimate judge of whether the criticism is destructive or constructive.
- Criticism and the manner in which it is conveyed depend on the objective and intention.
- Destructive criticism is the worst kind of criticism.
- Walk away from destructive criticism as much as possible.
- Constructive criticism can also sting, however, it is aimed at the improvement of a person or situation especially when that intention is clear enough.
- Knowing the difference between constructive and destructive criticism will result in the appropriate reaction to it.
- Always keep an open mind when receiving constructive criticism as you can gain useful tips, insights, and skills in the process.
- Don't internalize any kind of criticism. Simply choose a reaction and be open to learning from its outcome.
- We all make mistakes and can easily regret our destructive criticism in moments of anger, so forgive and be willing to work through issues effectively to neutralize strong emotions.
- As much as possible avoid any kind of criticism, rather offer feedback aimed at a person's growth, if you can help it.

- Remember to avoid internal negative feedback when receiving destructive criticism.

Self-compassion is the best antidote to criticism, as you've already learned. However, it can be applied every day to every situation to bring about more self-love in our lives. In the next chapter, you will learn more about the transformative power of self-compassion.

CHAPTER 6

SELF-COMPASSION

Allow the gentleness of your own compassion to touch your soul, as you navigate through life in all its richness, perplexes, and unpredictability.
–Marcee Martin

Understanding the Concept of Self-Compassion

Just as you would treat a friend or a soulmate in need of compassion, or just as you would embody the value of compassion to your child who is unfairly judging themselves, You owe it to yourself to express self-compassion every day in every moment of your life. Every one of us needs a dose of self-compassion because life can be rough, messy, and perplexing.

We all come from different backgrounds: cultural, ethnic, and religious. This may complicate things for us especially when it comes down to accepting that we are worthy of self-love, self-compassion, and self-forgiveness. Some of us have been brought up to be strong sister soldiers, always on duty faithfully taking care of everyone else: putting their needs first, and accepting second place when it comes to fulfilling your needs or checking in with yourself to see how you are doing.

Perhaps, you were brought up in a compassionate and loving home that supported your individual needs and taught you the importance of addressing your needs as a priority. Still, we are all sometimes guilty of neglecting to be more compassionate to ourselves, every day. The practice of self-compassion is transformative and powerful, it can change things for you.

By nature, most of us are hard on ourselves, especially during times when we need to be kinder. The darkness of regret, pain, envy, disappointment, or self-neglect can creep up on you when you least expect it to. You must guard against this, more so when your estrogen levels start declining, as you are more susceptible to mood swings when this starts happening. A lack of self-compassion can lead to many negative consequences for you, such as a lack of motivation, inner joy, an inability to be sociable, and mostly fear.

Reflect on your former years: Did anyone teach you to be more compassionate towards yourself? Or were the lessons based on the importance of accepting criticism rather than exercising self-compassion?

Why Are Most People Not More Compassionate to Themselves?

Women with very low self-esteem tend to shy away from practicing self-compassion. If you feel undeserving of living a brighter and happier life during midlife, then learning how to be more self-compassionate is one the first lessons you need to embrace willingly? It will also make you more loving, and improve your self-esteem. Without self-compassion, you will struggle on so many levels to love and appreciate yourself and to spread your wings in new directions.

Here's the thing about self-compassion: It really doesn't matter if you're having a good day or a bad day, a good daily dose of self-compassion is essential to get all things done in a day. Self-compassion is reflective of the amount of care you show to yourself in matters concerning every aspect of your life. It is forgiveness, love, and nurturing efforts all combined to manifest beautiful, more fulfilling results in your life. Practicing self-compassion really does matter to every woman, in midlife or not.

Be On Your Team First

We've all had those random moments of envy sneak up on us when we least expected them to. Or we may have rejected ourselves when we did not get the promotion we wanted or the job. How about the time when you noticed other women accomplishing things that you would've loved to accomplish? Envy is a subtle form of admiration, but lacking in self-compassion and it is a false feeling. It is unnatural to betray yourself, and your unique accomplishments. It may also be a sign that what you see in others is what you admire in yourself.

We've learned that we live in a competitive environment, so all the more reason to be on your team first!

It is a waste of energy to be envious. Rather focus on your strengths instead of beating yourself up because you failed to win someone else's approval of you. When we feel envy, it is a sign that we have failed to love ourselves enough regardless of whether we have lived up to the reputation of others. In those moments, self-compassion becomes relevant. It helps to neutralize emotions that are irrelevant and untrue. Any emotion that is linked to negating who you are and what you stand for is untrue. The truth is that you are always worthy of love, regardless of what you may or may not have done in your life.

Consider the times in your life when you came down hard on yourself: If you practiced more self-compassion how do you think your choices could've been different in the past? Use that wisdom now to apply it more every day to get new results!

_____

_____

_____

_____

_____

_____

_____

_____

_____

How to Turn Things Around When It Matters the Most to Our Morale?

We can choose to feel bitter about our perceived failures, or we can exercise compassion when experiencing envy, or jealousy by saying: "I really do admire her for her achievements, it resonates with my own values and ambitions, which are also in bloom to reflect my own unique position. I am happy for her outstanding achievements as I would be happy for my own, which are exemplary, and ever-evolving. There are lots of wonderful things that I have done to date that are most worthy of praise, as it required a great deal of effort on my part."

The negative emotions that come up for us, even if it is anger that we face, can also be neutralized by practicing more self-compassion. Being okay with things as they are is an act of self-compassion and self-acceptance. We cannot change the past, but we can certainly learn to accept past choices lovingly (by looking for hidden blessings) while being aware of new choices always on the horizon.

Importance and Impact of Self-Compassion

Remember Susan the Midlife-Globetrotter from Chapter 3? Well, Susan has shared some of her own insightful observations about the role that self-compassion can play in our lives. In one of her blogs, she shared how she finds herself admonishing herself for not completing projects. When she notices this, Susan immediately flips the switch from negative to positive by shining the light of self-compassion in the direction of those negative thoughts.

She turns the admonishing statement around immediately in her mind to reflect on the truth about her life. For example, when Susan became consciously aware of her earlier statement about never completing projects, she replaced it with the truth instead, "There are some projects that I have completed successfully and others that I have not, and that is okay." (Globetrotter, 2021, para. 6)

Self-compassion has the power of changing our reality immediately. Another important tool you can use in moments of despair is to pause to examine what may have triggered your negative feelings, pain, or psychological discomfort. Hit the pause button, and take a few moments to reflect on what you are feeling. This is how the practice of mindfulness can transform our lives. Once you are aware of the trigger, start pouring the wisdom and healing light of self-compassion into those thoughts, feelings, and emotional turmoil. It will take some practice but it is necessary to start applying this today in your life.

How Will Self-Compassion Change My Life?

The results of practicing self-compassion are calming and cathartic, and your actions will substantially reduce the chances of any negative thoughts or feelings spiraling completely out of control. Tell yourself that you are a kind-hearted and loving individual who is more than capable of overcoming any obstacles, and pain and that you deserve happiness, and can transcend this moment.

Quieten your mind, place your hands on your heart, and send love and compassion to yourself as you would comfort someone you love dearly. The focus on your high priorities for the day. When you nurture and focus on high-priority actions, you will reduce the chances of low priorities getting in the way. These high-priority actions will also fill your day with activity to keep your mind busy, productive, stimulated, and inspired.

The Components of Self-Compassion

a) **Self-Generosity or Avoiding Criticism of Yourself** This is a core component of practicing self-compassion. Just as Susan turned around her criticism to constructive feedback when she erroneously criticized herself for "never completing projects," so can you. Upon closer examination, Susan realized that there were some projects that she didn't complete and others that she did, and that was okay. When you examine your triggers of negative thoughts just as Susan did- you will see that criticism can be skewed based on emotions (Globetrotter, 2021).

b) **Your Humanity and Level of Empathy** The same considerate humanity that you display to others is required of you to generously display towards yourself, especially when challenged in any way. You are just as deserving as the next person. When we show empathy and compassion towards others, it is comforting to the person on the receiving end. This is how we connect to others at a heart level, and this should therefore be applicable to you.

c) **The Practice of Mindfulness** This is key to remaining objective, poised, and truthful when facing emotional upsets or strong negative emotions. Just calm yourself down, and examine those feelings, and emotions as an observer. The practice of mindfulness will get you to a place of objectivity, to address those triggers as you would do with a child in need of compassion and love. Mindfulness will help you to transcend those negative, conflicting moments. It will afford you the gift of self-compassion. (Summers, n.d.)

The Benefits of Self-Compassion

Good Health, Happiness, and Better Choices

Practicing self-compassion will improve how you feel about yourself, uplift you in moments of self-doubt, and leave you feeling totally in touch with your humanity. This in turn promotes good health as it reduces unnecessary stress in your life. You will in turn make better choices for yourself.

Healthy Self-Esteem

A healthy self-esteem is defined by your willingness to accept yourself as being human, and therefore you also accept that perfection is a state of being authentic. Healthy self-esteem is experienced when you are comfortable in your skin, your journey, your personal identity, and the choices you've made in life. Self-compassion when practiced daily, can bring you to experience this state of healthy self-esteem.

Promotes Resilience

Self-Compassion is a strength as it allows you to bounce quickly from setbacks in life. Self-compassion, therefore, promotes resilience, which is the ability to constantly transcend things. You will not be stuck for months, or even years following a challenging event because you had an emotional reaction to a situation that you could not beat! Emotional reactions that are strongly negative keep us stuck because we have not been kinder to ourselves.

Improves Your Humanity

Your sympathy for others will also increase when you are more self-compassionate. Connecting to people at a heart level is key to enjoying better, more authentic relations with them. Self-compassionate people are more giving, kinder people as opposed to being closed-off to themselves and others, and not being able to relate to people.

Self-Compassion Versus Self-Indulgence

Many people mistakenly believe that self-compassion is the same thing as being self-indulgent. On the contrary, while self-care is an important component of self-love and therefore also an act of kindness, it is not necessarily equivalent to self-indulgence. The latter is more of an escape route from confronting things head-on. Self-indulgence can be a way out of experiencing pain.

Self-compassion on the other hand is aimed at removing emotional turmoil or other negative factors in your life. Self-compassion is therefore about being kinder, and introspective, rather than attempting to ignore anything that may be challenging you. An example of being self-indulgent might be binge-watching on your favorite streaming channel or binge eating or taking a luxury holiday to escape not feeling good about yourself.

Self-indulgence may be a good idea for escapism to relax, unwind, and spoil yourself every now and then. However, it should not be mistaken for self-compassion as explained in the preceding paragraphs. Even though it is possible to combine being self-indulgent and self-compassionate at times, it is not the solution to being kind to yourself consistently.

Do keep in mind though, there is also a fine line that you should avoid crossing when being self-indulgent. It can be a negative factor and work against you if you keep turning to it for escapism. For example consuming too much champagne, unhealthy foods, and not attending to your nurturing self-care needs as a midlife woman is behavior that reflects negligence and not self-compassion.

You Do Not Have to Be Self-Indulgent to Be Self-Compassionate

It is not about indulgence but more about being kind, loving, and attentive to your emotional, psychological, and biological needs. Caring for yourself in all areas of your life without exercising personal judgment that attacks your self-esteem is the proper way of experiencing self-compassion. Having a pity party about your losses is also not an act of self-compassion.

Acceptance is at the heart of practicing self-compassion. You are allowed to be a normal human being who experiences emotions, as that is part of our humanness. Feeling happy or sad is what it is. When we attach labels to it, and are incapable of examining the root cause of our emotional discomfort, we get stuck. Often the views we hold about ourselves are skewed and when examined closer can be rectified to get us unstuck. As long as we find it within ourselves to rectify self-pity, and self-criticism appropriately by shining the light of truth on those negative emotions we will overcome any setbacks, and keep moving forward in the direction of the things we love.

Self-compassion is the compass of self-love, and self-acceptance is the destination of developing healthy self-esteem. This is also why you are here at this important phase in your womanhood to change old habits and seek a new lifestyle that is more supportive of your journey now in the second Spring of your life. Self-compassion is key to unlocking this change and your greatest adventure yet.

Making Self-Compassion a Way of Life

Making self-compassion a part of your daily life is not complicated at all. It is also about flipping the switch from being negative to positive. However, it also requires introspection and addressing emotions head-on realistically. Self-compassionate behavior directs us to self-love: To be kinder, and more loving to ourselves we can shine the light on who we truly are instead of succumbing to momentary feelings of inadequacy. Here's how to accomplish this daily.

1. Pause to reflect on strong negative emotions or thoughts that reflect a one-sided perspective to events, or labels you attach to your self-identity.
2. For example: If you are working on a project that is taking longer than usual and notice a negative self-judgmental

thought passing through your mind. Nip it in the bud. Do the same for any other judgemental negative thought that enters your mind in any situation.

3. Examine the negative judgmental statement or label you've attached to yourself, and upon closer inspection notice how generalized, exaggerated, and untrue it is. You are just having a passing negative emotional reaction. It is one-sided.

Make a list of all the negative judgemental labels you've attached to your self-identity in the past or present. Start questioning each one below by using self-compassion to remove those negative labels.

1.	
2.	
3.	
4.	
5.	
6.	
7.	
8.	
9.	
10.	
11.	
12.	
13.	
14.	
15.	

16.	
17.	
18.	
19.	
20.	

Key Takeaways

- The practice of self-compassion is transformative and powerful.
- A lack of self-compassion can lead to negative consequences such as a lack of motivation, inner joy, an inability to be sociable, and mostly fear.
- Mainly women with very low self-esteem tend to shy away from practicing self-compassion.
- Without self-compassion, you will struggle on so many levels to love and appreciate yourself and to spread your wings in new directions.
- Self-compassion is reflective of the amount of care you show to yourself in all matters concerning every aspect of your life.
- Self-compassion manifests into beautiful, more fulfilling results in your life.
- Practicing self-compassion will improve how you feel about yourself, and uplift you in moments of self-doubt.
- Self-compassion is a strength as it allows you to bounce quickly from setbacks in life.
- Self-compassionate people connect better with others, at a heart level, and therefore have healthier relationships.

In the next chapter, I will now help you relate better to self-criticism which is not an act of self-love or self-compassion. It is important to understand self-criticism a little more and to pause to reflect on why it has become such an integral part of our lives. Is it possible to let this go completely? Find out more in the next chapter.

CHAPTER 7

UNDERSTANDING THE DIFFERENCE BETWEEN SELF-CRITICISM AND SELF-REFLECTION

Beware of reaching out for perfection, when being good enough is your best and most important contribution. You are enough! –Marcee Martin

Self-Criticism

Make your list: Write down all the self-critical negative statements about yourself that you've entertained over the years and as you do, contemplate how each one stood in the way of living an extraordinary life.

1.	
2.	

3.	
4.	
5.	
6.	
7.	
8.	
9.	
10.	
11.	
12.	
13.	
14.	
15.	
16.	
17.	
18.	
19.	
20.	
21.	
22.	
23.	
24.	
25.	

26.	
27.	
28.	
29.	
30.	
31.	
32.	
33.	

Kicking the Habit of Self-Criticism

I can't think of a better time, than now at midlife, to get rid of all the self-criticism you've subjected yourself to over the years. There are so many women just like myself, who have experienced that internal ticking clock letting us know that life has flown by so fast yet surprisingly we remain stuck in old thinking patterns. The one most striking commonality that both men and women experience during their midlife transition is questioning their deepest beliefs and life choices. While you're doing this make a note to kick the habit of self-criticism, a negative habit of denying yourself peace, clarity, and personal fulfillment. As you probably realized from the preceding exercise, self-criticism is a joy killer.

Self-criticism is what it is: Nagging negative thoughts that we create and entertain because most of us are wounded emotionally, suffering from low self-esteem, while dealing with a barrage of issues that we allowed to invade our sacred space over the years. Self-criticism is negative self-talk that is strongly associated with the feeling of never being good enough.

Self-criticism left unchecked will rob you of experiencing more peace, love, and harmony in your life.

Feelings of not being good enough are often linked to deeper issues that have caused us to feel unworthy, alone, inferior, not beautiful, or even intelligent. For example, if you're struggling financially, those feelings will emerge even stronger; if you've suffered from a terrible break-up with a partner, those feelings will naturally emerge, and when we experience failure of any kind, those feelings also take on a heightened sensation.

Self-criticism and feelings associated with it, are usually triggered by events that have occurred in your life that you don't feel good about or when you unfairly judge yourself. It also originates from having internalized harsh criticism from family, friends, or others in our close-knit community. If you were criticized for not being smart enough in comparison to others you may have internalized it as being the truth. Once you examine closely the list you created on self-critical statements, you will notice that some of them may have had a lasting impact on your choices. (Golden, 2019)

Self-Reflection

There is a marked difference between self-criticism and self-reflection. Being self-reflective about your life is a positive quality. It allows you a chance to objectively evaluate your choices based on your level of consciousness in the past as compared to the present. Life is a journey of experiences, and each experience creates a shift of awareness. This is the natural outcome of growing and learning. Therefore self-reflection helps us to ascertain our past choices and experiences based on our level of growth.

For example, when you write and journal answers to the questions provided in this workbook, you are reflecting on your level of growth based on the transition you're experiencing at midlife. In the process of working through these practical exercises, you are also questioning, and evaluating what worked in the past and what is no longer working for you now. The objective self-reflection process will in turn lead to new insights, and realizations, and may even result in significant breakthroughs. Self-reflection allows us to look at the big picture of our lives, without judgment, and in the process, we also heal and learn to accept the choices we made in the past.

When we notice the negative patterns, a breakthrough may occur and we can in turn shift our behaviors accordingly. The midlife transition is therefore an important one of growing from all experiences through a process of self-reflection and self-evaluation. When we add the self-love bug to the process, we can heal, and limit judging ourselves negatively. Self-reflection is also an important process to reflect on past achievements, growth outcomes, and future goals and objectives.

Another way of considering self-reflection is thinking of it as a way of providing constructive feedback to yourself about your life's journey. Only when we reflect on our life can we make better choices for the present and the future? Therefore self-reflection provides us with a wide scope to self-evaluate our journey. Think of it as watching back the movie of your life, to determine where you need to correct certain behaviors about yourself, toward yourself, and your goals, to improve on the results you wish to obtain. Self-reflection and thus self-evaluation will give you the answers you are looking for in your midlife years, to create the ultimate blueprint for your next phase (Golden, 2019).

Identify through self-reflection how you can reverse the limiting beliefs you've held about yourself in the past.

The Differentiating Factors Between Self-Reflection and Self-Criticism

Understanding the Difference Between Destructive and Productive Self-Reflection

Just as you get constructive and destructive criticism you may find yourself embracing either one when undergoing a process of self-reflection. There is a difference between destructive and productive self-reflection. When you are objective in your approach to your journey of self-reflection you stand a better chance of achieving insightful breakthroughs as you are doing it as an act of self-love and not fear.

The idea is to observe objectively your past choices, behavior, and choices, to get the root cause of them, and to better understand yourself, and to shift your behavior as well as your thoughts accordingly. When you are less judgmental and more of an objective observer you will be able to affect meaningful change in your life.

Benefits of Self-Reflection Summed Up

- Allows for object self-evaluation of past thoughts, behavior, and choices based on belief systems.
- Creates shifts in awareness to help you make new improved choices, to achieve new desired results in your life.
- Limits the chances of repeating old negative thoughts and behavior patterns.
- Helps you to make new choices based on growth outcomes that you are seeking to experience.
- Allows you the chance to remove toxicity in areas of your life that have been negatively impacted by limiting beliefs and values.

- Will help you to create new beliefs and a new value system to support your new midlife transition.

How and Why You Should Switch From Self-Criticism to Self-Reflection

- Self-criticism destroys motivation, inspiration, and self-esteem.
- Self-criticism is an unhealthy way of undermining who you are, your experiences, and your growth outcomes.
- Self-criticism will also reduce the possibility of making new choices to support your new objectives.
- Self-criticism will keep you stuck in negativity.

The Impact of Self-Reflection

Overall, self-reflection will improve your ability to consistently evaluate your progress and allow you to make better, more productive, and positive choices for yourself. Self-reflection is a powerful way of healing from toxicity and negative patterns. The more you reflect on your choices the greater your ability to improve them and to consistently grow from those experiences.

It reduces the chance of being judgmental and increases the possibilities of achieving your new desired midlife goals and the outcomes you are seeking now in life. Finally, self-reflection will improve your psychological health as you hold yourself more accountable for your own choices in a way that upholds self-love in everything that you do, honorably, with compassion, and a willingness to overcome all challenges constructively.

Choose one specific area of your life, for example, romantic relationships or your career, and evaluate the patterns of your choices, behavior, and motivation. **Now write down the insights you've gained from this exercise below:**

Key Takeaways

- The one most striking commonality that both men and women experience during their midlife transition is questioning their deepest beliefs and life choices.
- Avoid self-criticism at all costs when evaluating your life's journey.
- Self-criticism is a joy killer!
- Self-reflection builds you up and boosts self-esteem, self-confidence, and self-respect.
- Being reflective is a positive quality. It helps you to improve in all areas of your life.
- Self-criticism can severely limit your chances of engaging in new possibilities.
- Self-criticism is what it is: Nagging negative thoughts that we create and entertain because most of us are wounded emotionally, and suffering from low self-esteem.
- Self-criticism is negative self-talk that is strongly associated with the feeling of never being good enough.
- Self-criticism is usually triggered by events that have occurred in your life that you don't feel good about.
- Self-criticism also occurs when you unfairly judge yourself.
- Self-criticism is an unhealthy way of undermining who you are, your experiences, and your growth outcomes.

In the next journey you will understand what it means to begin your journey of self-love; Where it begins and how it unfolds depends on your willingness to transcend negativity, and embrace a new brighter vision of your life.

CHAPTER 8

STARTING YOUR SELF-LOVE JOURNEY

Life is a kaleidoscope of memories that bear testament to a life well-lived.
–Marcee Martin

Taking Your First Steps Toward Self-Love as a Midlife Woman

I have no doubt in my mind that you are a very determined woman! You have made it this far in my book dedicated to healing your life from the inside out. That means that you are serious about changing your life. This is what healing with self-love is all about: changing your life, releasing toxicity, and reclaiming your full power, passion, and purpose. Life gets busy and somewhere in between all the important roles you've had to play throughout your womanhood, it is easy to neglect yourself, forget the nature of your true essence as a woman, and feel depressed about getting older.

It kind of piles up doesn't it? I know exactly what that feels like. This is why I was very determined to let all that go and I was fed up feeling depressed about the years I wasted feeling depressed! I may not have gone through a major depression but I experienced self-doubt, anxiety, and feelings of inadequacy. However, when I decided that change was necessary I pulled out the stops to make it happen!

I was determined to take the bull by the horns (get into action), and I jumped on the self-help bandwagon before any doubt entered my mind. I created the mind shift that was necessary to bring about that change in my life then jumped right into action. Deciding to make changes, committing to the journey, and jumping into action were the first few steps that I took toward self-love.

Here's the thing about midlife being a big wake-up call: It will suddenly dawn on you that you need change, and you will know intuitively what that change should be. You most likely have some idea about the change you want to experience in midlife like Theresa did when she turned 50.

Meet Theresa St. John

She married very young, way too young for her liking. Theresa St. John was only 18 years old when she had her first son. When she was 20 years old, she had her youngest son. In no time at all her marriage was in pieces. However, Theresa persisted in trying to make things work out. She had no other options at 20. At least that is what she thought at the time. She opted in and lasted for 15 long years in her marriage. It was mostly hard on her. Then one day, she got the nerve to think that there might be something better out there for her. She wanted to give it a shot.

Theresa started dating again. She had a ball of a time and worked hard as a single mum. She loved her two sons to the moon and back, and somehow they made it work as a family. Nine years into the dating scene and Theresa fell in love again. The warning signs were there, but she ignored them. Many years passed by until she admitted to herself that it was wasted years trying to bail out a gambler partner all the time.

It hit her hard when she lost everything she owned, including all her jewelry. By this time she was working three jobs at a time to pay the bills. Her gambling partner watched her struggle to keep things going for them as he wasted paycheck after paycheck. Finally, when she admitted that she couldn't take it any longer, he admitted to her that it was hard for him because he didn't "dislike her." She was appalled by his reaction and thought immediately of things like salmon, avocado, and winter. "He didn't dislike me like those things!" That was the final straw. It broke her back, and after yet another 15 years of marriage, she'd had enough. It was this motivation that kick-started her midlife transition.

Theresa's Midlife Transition

Theresa was 50 years old by now. She decided to fight harder for herself. She wanted to concentrate on herself. Clearly, the hormonal changes also kicked in and her new focus was completely on herself. As a result of this turning point in her life, Theresa shook things up and became very determined to change her life. After all, half a century had passed and she was done taking care of other people, especially men.

Theresa's determination in midlife saw her working harder, playing harder, and being smarter about her choices. She made a career change, and her motivation was no longer about just paying the bills. She took up photography after realizing her love for it, and she also decided that she was going to travel! Theresa signed up for some workshops and became the best student she could be for herself and her new career pursuits. By the time Theresa turned 56 she was a world traveler and international photographer.

What Theresa needed when she turned 50 were new goals and major change. That was her healing journey. She just knew what she wanted to do and she got straight into action doing it. Today she says she can still kick herself when reflecting on the years behind her. The only good things were her sons who gave her purpose back then. However, when she looks ahead she is excited about her life. She travels around the world with her Canon, sometimes alone, and sometimes with friends. She loves her new life (John, 2014).

What is the biggest psychological challenge you are facing right now in your life, and what do you think you need to do to heal from this? What does your intuition say to you?

___

___

___

___

___

___

___

___

___

Commit to the Change You Need in Your Life

If you are feeling low, depressed, and uncertain about your prospects at midlife, fear not. By reading through this book and working through these exercises you have taken your first few steps towards self-love and the more steps you take every day will pile up to replace those nagging fears, anxiety, negative thoughts, and stress. What you have to gain out of this book and your efforts, you will thank me for once you start implementing new actions every day in your life.

That's right you will get a new life, and a new outlook, you might even change the way you see the world, once you start believing in yourself again. Just as Theresa did, maybe you too will see more of the world if traveling is also one of your new goals. The thing about reaching this important milestone is the determination that follows once you decide on what you want out of life. Turning 50 can be a very empowering time, and if you've gone beyond 50 then NOW is also just as empowering as it will ever be, once you decide that it is.

Healing though does require patience, and a certain degree of enjoyment. It is a process of undoing years of negative thinking, and replacing them with a more balanced perspective on your life, its lessons, and your personal well-being. The latter once again is linked to following a daily self-care practice to get you feeling healthy, more peaceful, and open to new possibilities. That's where the enjoyment factor will kick in.

Healing is a process of enjoyment, mixed with reflective awareness and interspersed with moments of bliss as you reach within yourself, to truly unite all those broken pieces from the past to feel whole, and inspired from within. You will achieve more and more clarity as you work towards releasing toxicity from your life and embracing a more loving, compassionate, and brighter perception of yourself.

What Your Midlife Journey Is All About

This journey is all about YOU, the most important person in your life. If you do not mend your relationship with yourself now, you risk continuing down that same negative spiral of regret, low self-esteem, low self-acceptance, and low self-respect. However, if you continue to explore your new journey as Alice did in Wonderland, you will get "more curious" about all the new possibilities you can embrace, YES in midlife.

The first step is about taking action because once you've decided to make changes in your life, you must act immediately on the changes that are essential to make. I am hoping that you've worked through all the practical exercises in the preceding chapters and that you've been very productive already releasing negative issues and facing your challenges head-on. Journaling also helps to track your progress and to assess all your ideas properly. Eventually, you will be empowered to draw up a complete, and accurate plan of action, one that is an authentic representation of where you are now in your midlife journey.

The first step is always the most challenging to get through because you must do the work to see the changes you desire. This is especially true if you have a lot of pent-up emotions to work through at first. Sometimes, those pent-up emotions create psychological blocks for us. So don't skip any of the practical exercises here, you will achieve a lot if you work through all of them. It will help you identify where discomfort arises for you, so you can then proceed to start unwinding that negative ball of emotion that is attached to all unresolved issues.

Take your time if you need to when working through unresolved issues. Your goal should be to dissolve them so they no longer create psychological discomfort. It is possible to achieve this as long as you are willing to follow a self-care routine daily, and consistently work on releasing toxicity in your life. Work on yourself over the next 30 days consistently and you will experience results. There will undoubtedly be some shift that will occur on some level to influence you positively.

Your 30-Day Miracle

If you stick to this journey for 30 days, you will reap the rewards of your persistence. The first phase does require you to focus and pay attention to everything going on inside of you and in your life that requires fixing, healing, and self-love. You must open up to yourself first, and own your truth, what you are feeling and going through emotionally, and psychologically. Decide if you need to speak to a professional therapist. It can help, especially if you need a boost to deal with extremely toxic issues. It can be very comforting and reassuring to have a qualified professional therapist showing you the way to your stronger self.

Finally, at the end of this chapter, you must create a new routine for yourself that will include all the self-care practices that you are going to implement in your life. Sounds like too much all at once? No problem. Let's begin with understanding the mentality shift that is required of you to change your approach to midlife and your own personal development.

Understanding the Power of Self-Development and the Mentality Shift

What Does Self-Development Mean for Midlife Women?

Theresa St. John in the story above immediately knew that she wanted more from life when her second marriage came to an end when she turned 50. A crisis can lead to many enlightening new thoughts about yourself. This is why it is important to carefully examine the benefits of a crisis before choosing to crumble and abandon yourself in the grief process. For Theresa, the benefit of her second divorce was finally owning up to what she chose to ignore, the red flags in her relationship. Theresa overlooked that her husband was a gambler and it cost her dearly. She lost everything before she found herself again.

The hidden blessing for Theresa was that she realized that there was so much more to her than being married to a compulsive gambler who left her in a pile of debt. She wanted to pursue her passion for photography and decided to invest her time and resources to master the skill properly. Self-development for Theresa was therefore linked to her passion and authentic calling to take up photography as a career. She went from juggling three jobs to pay the bills to choose a soul-satisfying career (John, 2014).

At the core of self-development is self-love. When you fill your day with activities that you love doing, you will prosper and thrive in that vocation. Love is an important ingredient for everything in life and self-development in midlife must therefore be linked to what you love doing with your time. Choose an area of interest that excites you, and that makes you wake up every morning with the determination to succeed, thrive, and realize your greatest potential. Determination and a plan of action are the two important ingredients for your success.

The Importance of Self-Development in This Stage of Life

The midlife transition comes with a whole new outlook on life, and as mentioned a few times already, one of the changes that many midlife women encounter is making new career choices. It is as good as investing in a good holiday. Learning and developing your skills in midlife is worth the ride and the investment because it is often linked to enjoyable new opportunities for further growth.

You can grow and develop your current skills by learning new things, be a business owner, or a freelancer, or like Theresa and Susan the Midlife Globetrotter, you can travel around the world on your own terms. Both these women put their skills to good use and achieved so much for themselves in the process. Turning 50 did not stop them in their tracks to question their prospects. They decided on their midlife careers and went ahead to create and explore new career opportunities for themselves.

Your brain will love your new journey of self-development and will soon be firing and wiring new circuits as you learn new things to replace the humdrum ways of the past, negative thought patterns, and limiting beliefs. Personal empowerment is linked to personal development, and that brings us to discuss the three most important elements of self-development (Randolph, 2019).

Determining Your Passion

Now is the fun part of this chapter. You will begin assessing your past career and determine specific areas of interest to explore as a new potential career, hobby, or lifestyle.

1. Examine your past career choices. List them and write down how you feel about those accomplishments.

_____

_____

_____

_____

_____

_____

_____

_____

_____

_____

_____

_____

_____

2. Write down the skill set you've achieved throughout your professional life. For example, typing, teaching, making videos, running a successful cafe, etc.

3. Do you feel a strong desire to stick with the career path that you are following? Expand on your yes and no answer.

4. What are some of the other areas of interest that you've neglected or did not have the confidence in the past to pursue? If money was not an option would you pursue these interests and why?

title:	Self-Love Workbook for Midlife Women: A 12-Week Healing Journey; Release Toxicity, Overcome Self-...
Cond:	Good
User:	robbin_m
Station:	DESKTOP-8SELUVJ
Date:	2025-04-18 19:24:57 (UTC)
Account:	Blue Vase Books
Orig Loc:	Aisle 20-Bay 4-Shelf 1
mSKU:	BVM.4OUH
vSKU:	BVV.BOG6WTVVX.G
Seq#:	1062
unit_id:	28846588
width:	0.60 in
rank:	365,983
Cond	The item shows wear from consistent use, but it remains in good condition and works perfectly. All pages and cover are intact (including the dust cover, if applicable). Spine may show signs of wear. Pages may include limited notes and highlighting. May NOT include discs, access code or other supplemental materials.
Note:	

BVV.BOG6WTVVX.G

delist unit# 28846588

XXXXX

Millipn for Workbook for Whitten
Gailey/Davis Week 25 A paramig
Analytical Regular Yearbout
Overview Set

Cond.	good
Type	Paperback
Stock#	14113561753211
ISBN	9780534174378 (? 10 digit)
Author	Ann Liby Book
Pub Date	4 days 4 Apr 02 Display
List...	PAM HOUSE
ASIN	5XAALWAGQAA1
Skus	1005
Pu...	0535895
Wi...	10.09.0
Loc...	L45 605

© XXX MANAGAL/XAM

5. If you are still interested in sticking to your current profession then explore areas for further self-development and get excited about how you can advance your career in midlife.

Key Takeaways

- Deciding to make changes, committing to the journey, and jumping into action are the first few steps to self-love.
- The thing about reaching this important milestone is the determination that follows once you decide on what you want out of life.
- Turning 50 can be a very empowering time, and if you've gone beyond 50 then NOW is also just as empowering as it will ever be!
- Healing does require patience, and a certain degree of enjoyment. It is a process of undoing years of negative thinking, and replacing them with a more balanced perspective on your life, its lessons, and your personal well-being.
- Take action on your goals once you've reached clarity!
- You must act immediately on the changes that are essential to implement.
- Take your time to work through unresolved issues. Your goal should be to dissolve those unresolved issues so they no longer create psychological discomfort for you.
- Stick to your healing journey for 30 days, you will reap the rewards of your persistence.
- You must open up to yourself first, and own your truth.

In the next chapter you will learn more about self-esteem and how to improve it.

CHAPTER 9

THE THREE HORSEMEN OF SELF-DEVELOPMENT

Let today be the day that you love yourself completely, and act on it in every way in your life!
—Marcee Martin

Learning All There Is to Know About Self-Esteem

Notice if you are experiencing any negative thoughts at present. How does it make you feel and what is the cause of these negative thoughts? Do you think you can go through one whole day without thinking any negative thoughts or feeling bad about anything in particular? Sometimes a lingering negative thought from an unresolved issue has a way of nagging us at the back of our minds, even when everything else is going smoothly. Watch out for those lingering, and persistent negative thoughts. Unless you heal it, work past it to let it go, it may persist until the next one comes along. Write down what is the cause of any persistent negative thoughts at the back of your mind today.

What is Self-esteem?

Self-esteem is how you feel about yourself. It is directly related to your state of psychological health and may be a good way to gauge how you are really doing as opposed to how you say you are doing when someone asks or how you think you are doing. Sometimes we can so easily deceive ourselves into believing that we are doing great when we are not. We may look great on the outside, but on the inside, there is always some lingering negative thought or residual energy of toxic energy that we are struggling to get past. I think for many years I went through one issue after another thinking if I could get past this one life will just be great.

The truth is hard to accept at times. We may look like we have great self-esteem, however, the truth may be that we could be at rock bottom in some ways while doing great in other ways. When we are sitting on a nail (in some kind of pain psychologically) it can override all the other feel-good factors. This is why it is important to start owning those positive traits and allow them instead to overshadow the negative, toxic thoughts that pull us down.

Your level of positivity will depend on how you feel about yourself. This is why self-love is an important way of healing and harmonizing your psychological state of wellness. A healthy dose of daily self-love will keep your self-esteem at a healthy functional level, regardless of challenges. Mindfulness will also ensure that you are consciously aware of the things that bug you psychologically. Meditation helps to pinpoint those areas that are affected by negative thoughts or troubling life events. As you already know, midlife does not need to be one of those negative events. That is why you are learning everything you need to know about midlife, so you can overcome issues of the new unknown in the midlife territory. You have got it covered now.

Tips to Improve Your Level of Self-esteem

Take note of these powerful tips to improve your level of self-esteem. As you read, keep in mind the remaining two horsemen of self-development: self-acceptance, and self-confidence. All three are interconnected and therefore need to be nurtured simultaneously.

1. **Focus On Encouraging, Constructive Thoughts as Opposed to Negative Ones**

    If you are having a bad day due to someone or something that occurred, reduce the tension by encouraging yourself that it will pass, occupy your mind with something else, or think of the big-picture vision of your life or you could pop out for a quick massage or lunch with a friend. Do something to turn around the lingering negative feelings. Avoid internalizing events and negative encounters.

2. **Goal Setting**

   Knowing where you are heading and having clarity on what you want to achieve in all areas of your life will give you real focus. Every determined and successful woman knows what she wants! This is a real self-esteem booster.

3. **Taking Care of Yourself**

   Don't neglect your diet or your self-care routine. Put on those running shoes, grab your iPod, and get moving. Feel the fresh air welcome you and embrace the NOW. Remember that you can simply decide to hit the pause button on those strong emotions. Just press pause and take care of yourself instead.

4. **Reduce Stress**

   No matter what is going on in your life, tell yourself that you deserve that yoga class or meditation session at the end of the day. The ball is always in your court about how you are feeling about your life. Don't allow stress to have its way with you. Keep yourself internally focussed and move towards your self-love goals always, especially when you need it the most.

5. **Look Back on Your Life, Especially Your Accomplishments**

   Feel proud about how far you've come in life, that you made it to midlife, and that you're still going strong with lots of inspiring goals set to achieve. Celebrate it more often. We often take for granted how hard it was in the past to achieve those important milestones. Remember all the sacrifices you made and how you've grown in the process to be the remarkable woman that you are today.

We've all had a ton of things to get through in life before we arrived at midlife. There were also tons of moments that we struggled to get through and maybe some of those moments extended into years. **List them here and consider what a waste of energy it was stressing over things that don't really matter at all today!**

What Is Self-Acceptance?

As a concept self-acceptance is easy enough to understand. It means that you totally and authentically accept yourself right now as you are, regardless of what you are doing to improve your life, and your experiences. Right now as you are, you are enough, blessed, beautiful, and abundantly talented. Self-acceptance means that even though you may have a ton of weight to lose before your next holiday you are happy within yourself, productive, and content about who you are on the inside and on the outside.

Say out loud, " Right now I have everything I need and I am content with who I am from the inside out. I am worthy of love no matter what I have done in the past or did not do." Now right down how you feel about loving yourself and accepting yourself at this moment. Also, reflect on how in the past you failed to accept yourself even though you had so much going for you. Make a promise to yourself that, as the greatest gift of self-love, you will always accept yourself completely, regardless.

_____

_____

_____

_____

_____

_____

_____

_____

_____

_____

_____

Why Does It Matter?

It matters for tons of reasons. Not only is it healing and cathartic to stop rejecting yourself, but it is also empowering to know that you do regardless of anyone else's opinion. Women just like men tend to compare themselves to others. There is no need for this. When you love and accept yourself, you will stop this unhealthy habit, and start feeling good in your own skin again. You will feel more confident about yourself, and simply be who you are without apologies. Most importantly you will stop putting others on pedestals, and start looking up to yourself.

It is unhealthy to put anyone on a pedestal, rather, put them in your heart and see them for who they really are: Another human being just like you who needs authentic love and acceptance. We are all going through things whether it is a midlife transition, financial crises, or a difficult pregnancy. Learning to accept ourselves will lighten the burden and improve our chances of getting through tough times. When you accept yourself it is also easier to be honest with yourself about your challenges, and simply be in the moment, working through stuff to get to the other side of it.

When you accept yourself, you know in your gut that things are exactly as they are because of the choices you made and that you can change anything in time with persistence, patience, and powerful new intentions. You will also take rejection less personally, and stand your ground when it is required. That too is an act of self-love. Self-acceptance is a manifestation of self-love. You are choosing yourself and you know that is the best choice to make in all circumstances (Perera, 2020).

What Benefits Does It Give You as a Midlife Woman?

The best part about self-acceptance for midlife women is that it will liberate you from the toxicity of the past. All unresolved emotions keep us stuck in the past. When we decide to heal from them as you are doing now in this workbook, you are taking greater steps towards achieving complete self-acceptance. That is powerful, and it is shaping your mindset to be enthused about everything that is in front of you now. When you reach self-acceptance, it is like you are starting life on a clean slate. You are here with me on this powerful self-love healing journey because a part of you has struggled to accept the past, not the present.

Working through the past and making peace with your new midlife journey is going to heal you profoundly. Most of the time in midlife we are looking behind us and not in front of us. This is the grieving process that most women go through. However, the view in the rearview mirror is always slightly skewed. You are bound to experience discomfort. Reaching self-acceptance will prepare you for what lies ahead in a way that is truly inspiring, with a wider view and perspective on life.

Write down all the things about yourself that are difficult to accept right now, then start reframing your mind around these areas to support the necessary healing. Next to each characteristic or present trait come up with a solution. **Ask yourself: How can I make this quality more accepting?**

_____

_____

_____

_____

What is Self-Confidence?

When you wake up in the morning and you are ready to shine your light in the world, enthused to reflect your authenticity unashamedly; when you have a bounce in your step because it feels great to be alive, and to be you; when you know there is only one blueprint of you in the world, and that by itself is a cause for celebration. Self-confidence occurs when you feel a great amount of trust and belief in yourself, and your abilities. It is a healthy psychological state of being, one that we must strive to attain and maintain.

At this point I am also excited to mention that the next book in this series is about self-confidence, *The SELF CONFIDENCE workbook for MIDLIFE WOMEN: A 30-Day Self-Discovery Journey to Own Your SH*T and Reignite the Badass Woman That You Are*! Don't wait too long before you begin the next part of your journey with me, email me to be included in my VIP list. I promise to send you a copy of the second book before it is released to the public. Here is my email address: hello@marceemartin.com. Also, feel free to share with me details about your midlife struggles. I would love to hear from you.

Pause to reflect on how confident you feel today. Are you smiling from within your soul, and it feels wonderful to be you right now, all day? If not what is holding you back from feeling confident in yourself, your abilities, and your talents without knocking anyone else down?

_____

_____

_____

_____

Understanding the Fine Line Between Confidence and Overconfidence

Overconfidence often borders on narcissism. It occurs when you overestimate yourself as being better than others. It is not a healthy psychological state to be in, as you come across as someone who feels superior to others. Feelings of superiority and inferiority are both unhealthy psychological states. Real confidence occurs when you feel balanced from within, enthused and happy to be yourself, without any desire to push others down or to overstate your abilities. Real confidence cannot be faked as it is a state of experiencing inner peace, and self-acceptance.

Often narcissists display overconfidence because deep down they feel a lack within themselves, and therefore a need to display false confidence. A narcissist is someone who possesses a fragile ego and desires nothing more than to mask it to the world. Narcissism is a personality disorder. When you are confident authentically it does not come from any feelings of lack, but feelings of trust and belief in yourself. You also know instinctively that you are not perfect. However, your focus is on your strengths and guard against negativity.

Self-criticism does not feature strongly in the life of a confident person. A confident person embraces self-love completely in a healthy way and is also therefore committed to their self-care needs, which includes checking in with themselves regularly to see how they are really doing and working past moments of self-doubt or negative thinking. A self-confident person always leaves room for personal improvement, without seeking perfection, only excellence!

Take the Self-Confidence Quiz

Start your self-care practice today, and start prioritizing needs first. Ask yourself this question: What do I want? Don't stop asking this question every day and keep honoring the things that are important to YOU. Are you ready? Let's begin! (Thriving, 2022)

Go ahead and see how you score on this quiz, created by Empowered And Thriving in 2023. Answer honestly. In total, you will answer 20 questions. Select either Yes, Sometimes, or No in response to each of the questions below. The process to assess the results is included at the end of the quiz.

1. When I look at myself in the mirror or think about myself: I see my traits as being attractive and I don't think of my flaws much.

YES	SOMETIMES	NO

2. I don't hesitate to take a stand for myself when judged unfairly or taken advantage of.

| YES | SOMETIMES | NO |

3. I feel very comfortable in my skin and around others, I love my own style and being myself.

| YES | SOMETIMES | NO |

4. I make eye contact with others comfortably.

| YES | SOMETIMES | NO |

5. I am comfortable being the center of attention.

| YES | SOMETIMES | NO |

6. I am capable of handling new situations with ease.

| YES | SOMETIMES | NO |

7. I don't judge myself harshly and it is easy to let go of challenging situations.

| YES | SOMETIMES | NO |

8. I don't take criticism too personally and can handle it with an open mind.

| YES | SOMETIMES | NO |

9. I make decisions confidently and with ease, seldom second-guessing myself.

| YES | SOMETIMES | NO |

10. I express myself freely.

| YES | SOMETIMES | NO |

11. I don't worry about being judged as "incompetent."

| YES | SOMETIMES | NO |

12. I don't obsess about the past.

| YES | SOMETIMES | NO |

13. Rejection doesn't bother me much.

| YES | SOMETIMES | NO |

14. I am not overly interested in what people think of me.

| YES | SOMETIMES | NO |

15. I don't hesitate to see to my needs first asking for what is important to me.

| YES | SOMETIMES | NO |

16. I feel worthy of my life.

| YES | SOMETIMES | NO |

17. I accept compliments easily and they don't make me feel uncomfortable.

| YES | SOMETIMES | NO |

18. I accept my general appearance.

| YES | SOMETIMES | NO |

19. I am in total control of my fears and do not suffer from anxiety much.

| YES | SOMETIMES | NO |

20. I say "No" easily to things that do not appeal to me.

| YES | SOMETIMES | NO |

All "Yes" answers are equal to 2 points. You will earn 1 point for "Sometimes," and 0 points for a "No" answer. Calculate your total points based on your responses. Use that number to determine your self-confidence level from the scale below.

Self-Confidence Quiz Assessment

If your total is between 35–40 then you are a Guru! This means that you are confident in yourself and are constantly doing things to keep up your level of self-confidence. Keep on this trajectory and you will be rocking it!

If your total is between 24–34, you are a Beginner! This means you are doing well in the self-confidence space but there is still room for improvement! Keep up your self-love routine, and soon you will be a Guru!

If your total is between 0–23, then you are a Novice. This means that you are struggling to gain confidence in yourself, and you have some work to do!

Now, write down the new insights that you discovered about your level of self-confidence. Are you ready to do more work to raise your game? If so, what would that be?

_____

_____

_____

_____

_____

_____

_____

_____

_____

How Is Self-confidence Capable of Giving You a Positive Change in Midlife?

When you love and appreciate your unique traits and see yourself as so much more than just reaching perimenopause or menopause, you will feel more confident about your transition to midlife. You will also feel more capable of handling change. Being confident puts you in the control seat because you are not expecting perfect results all the time. You know how vitally important your attitude and choices will be to ensure a great midlife transition.

Hacks Boost Self-Confidence

Increasing Awareness Practicing mindfulness is an important way of keeping yourself grounded in the present moment. Self-awareness improves your relationship with yourself and will increase your level of confidence in your abilities to accomplish anything that you set your mind on. Focus on your thoughts and feelings throughout the day intermittently in a way that is non-judgmental.

Getting Through the Tough Times With a Steady Mindset Be steady and do not allow strong emotions to derail you. Stick with your self-care practice, and just keep believing in yourself even when things are tough.

Talking To Yourself Speak kindly to yourself, and remember to always flip that switch of internal dialogue from negative to positive. Say to yourself out loud, "I believe in me!" Do things that will reinforce your confidence, and accept yourself always in every moment unconditionally.

Surround Yourself With Positive and Inspiring People Keep the right company that will reinforce good feelings about yourself. Stay away from people who do not have your best interest at heart and are negative. The good energy will stick and help uplift you. There is nothing more inspiring than being in great company.

Dress Well Dress comfortably and always look neat and presentable in your own choice of fashion. This hack is easy to accomplish. Dressing well does increase confidence and you will feel great in all situations. (Thriving, 2023)

Key Takeaways

- Watch out for those lingering, and persistent negative thoughts. Unless you heal it and work past it to let it go, it may persist.
- Self-esteem is how you feel about yourself.
- Self-acceptance means that you totally and authentically accept yourself right now as you are, regardless of what you are doing to improve your life, and your experiences.
- Say out loud, " Right now I have everything I need and I am content with who I am from the inside out. I am worthy of love no matter what I have done in the past or did not do."
- Self-confidence occurs when you feel a great amount of trust and belief in yourself, and your abilities.
- Self-awareness improves your relationship with yourself and will increase your level of confidence in your abilities to accomplish anything that you set your mind on.
- Speak kindly to yourself, and remember to always flip that switch of internal dialogue from negative to positive.
- Say to yourself out loud *I believe in me.*
- Do things that will reinforce your confidence, and accept yourself always in every moment unconditionally.

You don't have to go through the rest of your life only identifying with your problems and challenges. Let's get rid of them in the next chapter.

CHAPTER 10

GETTING RID OF THE PROBLEMS ONE BY ONE

Our life is defined by the quality choices that we make and how we react to our problems.
–Marcee Martin

Problems That Live Beneath Your Personality

Identify your personality traits that make you uncomfortable. Do you know why?

_____

_____

_____

_____

_____

_____

Problems That You Might Be Suppressing

You may or may not know that you are suffering from a personality disorder or that there might be underlying issues that go beyond the hormonal changes occurring during midlife. For example, narcissists are unaware that they are suffering from low self-esteem issues, and sometimes trauma may have disrupted your normal behavior to some degree. There may be other times you start talking yourself into anxiety, and depression or you may be setting the scene for a "bad mood day."

Depending on what issues we may also be facing, it is difficult to tell if some of our neurotic behavior is caused by our personality. It was Karen Horney, a German-born psychologist who observed that people create their own misery at times. According to her, it occurs because of our personalities or traits that evolved into neurotic behavior. This neurotic behavior in turn has caused some people to behave in self-defeating ways. It is the deep underlying belief, according to Karen, that "you are not good enough, " which will keep you in the way of your own success (Whitbourne, 2021).

For example, if you believe that you are not worthy of love, regardless of how hard you try, this belief will self-sabotage your relationships, and you will adopt personality traits to match the ingrained belief. You may start creating conflict at a subconscious level to prove your belief right every time, by putting up more and more walls between you and your partner. These problems that arise from personality disorders, and behavior problems will cause you to distress more often than not, unless you understand them, and get to the root cause of them.

Measure Your Personality Problems

You can now rate yourself according to the *Interpersonal Problems Rating Scale* to assess what your underlying personality problems are. It was compiled under extensive research conducted by Michael Bordeaux and other researchers (Whitbourne, 2021). Once measured, you will have an idea of exactly what some of your personality issues are and their associated triggers. Awareness is always the first step towards healing a challenge. Rate your personality problems on a scale from 0-3 points for the following personality traits (0 for no problem, and 3 for serious problem):

1.	You get easily upset by little things.	
2.	You cry often when you are upset.	
3.	You often express anger through tantrums.	
4.	Others easily annoy you.	
5.	You have feelings of worthlessness or inadequacy take over often.	
6.	You often compare yourself to others.	
7.	You feel that others are better than you (better looking, richer, smarter).	
8.	You are very self-critical.	
9.	You have problems focusing.	
10.	You are easily distracted.	
11.	Uncertain about what you want from life.	
12.	You procrastinate often.	
13.	You lie often and even steal from others.	

14.	Infidelity is a common activity for you.	
15.	You take too many risks.	
16.	You have a problem following rules.	
17.	You have trouble being spontaneous.	
18.	You don't like taking chances.	
19.	You push yourself too hard to excel.	
20.	You strive for perfection.	
21.	You don't like trying new things.	
22.	You fantasize more than actually living your life.	
23.	You imagine things for the worst.	
24.	There is no excitement in your life.	
25.	You do not experience strong emotions.	

Here's what your scores tell you about yourself.

1. A score of 0–4 indicates emotional dysregulation. In other words, you have difficulty managing your emotions, and stress levels and you tend to feel frustrated very easily.

2. A score of 5–8 indicates that you tend to internalize things easily. This brings on sadness and uncertainty in your life.

3. A score of 9–12 indicates that you are easily distracted and struggle to focus on your tasks.

4. A score of 13–16 indicates that you act out and take risks more often. In other words, you tend to externalize your issues.

5. A score of 17–22 indicates that you are a perfectionist.

6. A score of 23–24 means that you fantasize a lot and tend to live there more than in reality.

7. Finally a score of 25–26 indicates apathy, a strong lack of interest or concern.

The above exercise most likely results in insightful discoveries about your hidden personality problems. This means that you are now one step closer to thwarting those problems from recurring in your life. The above result is reflective of your intrapersonal problems which most likely manifest in certain areas of your life. If you are seeing a pattern in behavior emerge when looking at your score, use that discovery to address ongoing issues that are relatable to that pattern. Now you know what you can start working on to get rid of your problems that are linked to this behavior (Whitbourne, 2021).

Draw a list of some of the common triggers that result in strong emotional responses or extreme behavior on your part.

1.	
2.	
3.	
4.	
5.	
6.	
7.	
8.	
9.	
10.	
11.	
12.	
13.	
14.	

15.	
16.	
17.	

Isolating the Problems and Solving Them One by One

1. **How to Avoid Feeling Overwhelmed by Thinking**

    A simple solution is to press the pause button when you find yourself caught in the web of endless thinking. Don't think your life away, it is meant to be lived to the fullest. Overthinking is a joy killer. If you have issues to deal with, then deal with them head-on by directly reaching new resolutions.

2. **Solving Depression and Anxiety**

    You can solve depression and anxiety through a combination of self-healing practices and professional treatment. It all depends on the severity of the problem. You will know instinctively the type of care that is needed for yourself, based on how it is affecting you in your everyday activities, relationships, and professional goals. However, once again, maintaining a solid routine of self-care will eliminate the causes much faster. Emotional self-care lies at the heart of preventing depression and anxiety from manifesting in deep psychological challenges.

3. **Getting Rid of the Worrying That You Do**

    Remember that all you have in a day is 24 hours. Most of us have wasted years worrying over things that ended eventually. Be in the moment, live in the moment, and let things take care of themselves. Trust in your ability to get through the things that are most meaningful to you every day, and let everyone else deal with their own stuff. Make yourself a priority and release negative thoughts, including worrying about things for the highest good to resolve itself in its own time. Deal with what you can and ensure that you are following a healthy, inspiring, and vibrant self-care routine daily.

4. Emptying Out Your Mind and Starting From a Fresh Canvas

Do this every day after your morning meditation, and leave yesterday's dramas where they belong, in the past. The art of practicing mindfulness is a brilliant way of simply releasing things that are not relevant to a new day. Each day know what your priorities are, and focus on getting them done, instead of carrying stuff over from yesterday or the past.

5. Getting Over Feelings of Inferiority

When you are not living a life that is congruent with the things you love occupying your time with, you can easily end up succumbing to feelings of inferiority. Set meaningful goals, exercise, upskill, and practice self-love daily. You will reap the gains of this, and those feelings of inferiority will soon pass. Fill your day with inspiring activities, do what you love, and most importantly flip the switch of internal chatter from negative to positive. If your feelings of inferiority are linked to criticism from others, then diminish the power of experiencing an extended emotional reaction, refer back to Chapter 7 and work through it once again.

6. Putting on the Right Mindset

The right mindset is one that prioritizes your needs, acknowledges that there are unique changes you are experiencing during your midlife transition, and consistently encourages you to move forward positively and enthused about this phase of your life. Embrace the magic of tiny steps and uphold the big vision of how you would love your life to unfold for you now. You've come through so much already over the years, midlife holds many promises for you. May it exceed your wildest expectations!

7. **Dealing With Romantic Relationships**

    Romantic relationships can pull us down or spice things up. Your partner should be a support pillar of love and encouragement to help through the midlife transition. Take the journey together and explore new ways of bonding. If there are red flags in your relationship, deal with them instead of turning a blind eye. Breakups, divorce, and major shifts in your romantic relationship are expected to occur at midlife. Everything really does change in midlife; your entire perspective is going to shift and keep shifting as you progress through perimenopause and menopause. Things that were once important may no longer seem relevant, and you will go through a phase where you will question the integrity of your relationships. So be prepared for anything, by trusting your heart, and following what feels right for you.

Pause to reflect on the quality of your relationships, especially with your partner and family members. Do you notice any new thought patterns emerging for you concerning these relationships?

Key Takeaways

- Depending on what issues we may also be facing, it is difficult to tell if some of our neurotic behavior is caused by our personality.
- People do create their own misery at times, so be aware of your personality traits, and behavior. Avoid self-sabotaging your own happiness.
- You may start creating conflict at a subconscious level to prove your belief right every time. Avoid this and be aware of the walls that come up for you in specific situations.
- If you are struggling with personality issues, get professional help if need be.
- It may be hard to accept that we have problems with our personalities that keep us stuck but most people do.
- If you find yourself overthinking issues, and creating more anxiety in the process, press the pause button.
- Don't obsess over your problems: Be in the moment, live in the moment, and let things take care of themselves.
- There are always solutions in front of you. Keep a level head, and you will be awakened to find solutions for every problem you encounter.
- Remember that you've gotten this far in life, so you know that there will be problems and there will be solutions. Nothing lasts forever.
- Release yesterday's problems and start each day on a clean slate.
- Leave the past where it belongs, worrying is a joy killer!
- Set meaningful goals, exercise, upskill, and practice self-love daily, you will beat feelings of inferiority this way.

Get ready to change your life by learning how to set meaningful boundaries in the next chapter.

CHAPTER 11

THE IMPORTANCE OF SETTING POSITIVE BOUNDARIES TO ACHIEVE SELF-LOVE

Every moment is a fresh new beginning.
−T.S. Elliot

Yale professor Becca Levy undertook detailed research that spanned decades to uncover how a person's beliefs about aging impact longevity, and even mortality. In a blog, she shared some of those startling discoveries, which made a lot of women pause to reflect on the state of their psychological health. Her research tracked middle-aged women for a period of 20 years. Professor Levy discovered that middle-aged women who were positive and embraced aging positively lived 7.5 years longer than those who were negative and pessimistic (Cabrera, 2022).

In another study, Levy tracked hundreds of adults for a period of 38 years and discovered that those who were positive with a brighter outlook on life also enjoyed better health and a lower risk of heart failure. Some of the other findings are as follows:

1. A lower risk of dementia.
2. Improved memory.
3. Better hearing and faster recovery from trauma.

To beautifully summarize her findings, Levy wrote about how positive people generally do things to support their development, recovery, and health. Self-care practices like following a healthy diet, exercising more, following their doctor's professional advice and reducing stress were all major contributing factors. When stress is reduced so is the negative impact of high levels of the stress hormone cortisol. On the other hand, adults held negative views about aging tested with higher levels of cortisol. This is, in turn, triggered by chronic stress, inflammation, and various illnesses like diabetes, Alzheimer's, and heart issues (Cabrera, 2022).

It is not difficult to flip that switch from negative to positive. Everything in this book is leading you down the path to enjoying better physical, emotional, and psychological health. Following a daily inspiring self-care practice, journaling, and practicing mindfulness, will all get you to a positive place in your life. Setting healthy boundaries is also a positive shift that you can make in your life today, which will totally liberate you from the negativity of others. Putting yourself first is at the core of the practice of self-love, and will get you on the road to good health in every conceivable way.

The Impact of Positive Boundaries

What Are Boundaries?

Knowing what pushes you to your limits in all situations is just as important as eating healthy, exercising, or meditating daily. Whatever it is or whoever it is that pushes those limits must be addressed to reduce the discomfort it causes you, as that is a stressor. Imagine if you had no boundaries and constantly gave all of yourself and everything to everyone in every situation.

The result will be exhaustion, a lack of focus, and less time for yourself. It is not possible to live happily this way for a number of reasons: You will be used, abused, taken advantage of, and disrespected. So you guessed correctly: Boundaries set us on a track that prioritizes you, and what is important to you. For example, if you are having intense relationship issues with family members then setting boundaries should include minimizing your time with them or coming up with a strategy that will let them know how you feel about spending too much time with them.

Unless there are firm resolutions and boundaries established to address the conflicting issues, the chances of ongoing discomfort in your life will continue to cause unnecessary stress in your life. Similarly, if you find that you tend to be a people pleaser at work, by always doing more than your share without recognition, compensation, or acknowledgment, then it is time to start creating and implementing healthy boundaries.

Maybe you do not feel good socializing beyond work with colleagues but have been feeling obliged to do so. Setting healthy boundaries by reducing your attendance at social events with colleagues outside work hours will be a healthy solution to this dilemma. Setting healthy boundaries that do not destroy relationships is essential to maintain them and to also reduce stress in your life. Effective communication lies at the heart of establishing boundaries. It can be achieved in a subtle way by simply declining invitations politely or making yourself unavailable at large family gatherings, if this is what brings you discomfort (Hailey, 2022).

What pushes your boundaries? Let's list them and get them out of our system, in this way we will respect our boundaries more, and know what to avoid, who to avoid, and how to handle these stressful situations better.

1.	
2.	
3.	
4.	
5.	
6.	
7.	
8.	
9.	
10.	
11.	
12.	
13.	
14.	
15.	
16.	
17.	
18.	
19.	

20.	
21.	
22.	
23.	
24.	
25.	
26.	
27.	
28.	
29.	
30.	
31.	
32.	
33.	
34.	
35.	
36.	

How Do They Help You Out?

When there are no healthy boundaries in place, there is bound to be psychological discomfort, resentment, inner turmoil, and unsatisfactory relationships. Just as is important to ensure a healthy boundary with your neighbors for example to maintain ongoing good neighborly relationships you must also set up metaphorical fences in every area of your life to ensure healthy, and supportive relationships as opposed to combative, unhealthy, and chaotic ones.

As you transition to midlife, reducing stress, drama, and chaos and eliminating negative aspects of your life are important. A lack of healthy boundaries will lead to manipulation, exploitation, coercions, and getting involved in projects or things that are of little interest to you. Knowing when to draw the line with people in various situations tactfully or at times assertively is a surefire way of establishing healthy relations and keeping yourself focused on what is important to you first and foremost.

If you have always been an accommodating person to others at a high cost to your own happiness, then it is time to determine what your limits are, and where you can set up healthy boundaries to have more time for yourself and your priorities. Learning to say "No" to those things that drain you and do not resonate any longer is an important part of creating a new lifestyle that is supportive of your self-love goals. Do not betray yourself by agreeing to things that your heart is not invested in.

Start Working on These Boundaries to Gain the Upper Hand in Situations

Here is a list of where you need to create boundaries in your life. It will help you to achieve clarity on issues that are unhealthy in your life, as well as associations with people that are inauthentic and stressful.

1. **Social Boundaries**

    Whether in your personal or professional life, your friends and colleagues need to know your boundaries. What they are, and why they are important to you? For example, going to nightclubs may not be your thing anymore but traveling around the globe with your family may be more important, enriching, and enlightening. You don't need to go to great lengths explaining yourself. Simply state what does not interest you and make alternate suggestions.

2. **Boundaries in Relationships**

   Communicating effectively with your partner, children, or other family members who make up your close inner circle of relationships are just as important. Healthy boundaries manifest into healthy, more loving, nurturing relationships with others. Let them know what you value and get to know you intimately through your open authentic communication with them. If you require time for some solo traveling for example, let your partner and family know why this is important to you, and go for it. Receiving love, support, and encouragement is a healthy way of developing and maintaining a healthy relationship.

3. **Boundaries in Your Emotional Kingdom**

   If you've recently got heartbroken, then boundaries in your emotional kingdom are important to set up. This means that you can decide how your relationship with the other person evolves, changes, and transitions. It will also include how you will engage in the future with other potential love interests. Maybe you were heartbroken because you rushed in without effectively communicating the things that are important to you, or you did not open up about certain things that you wanted to explore on your own. Make a list of new boundaries to prepare yourself to handle things better in the future.

4. **Creating Boundaries From Negative Emotions**

   Learn how to determine the triggers in your life that lead to you experiencing more negative emotions. Then start isolating yourself from those negative emotions. Earlier in Chapter 6, we discussed ways in which you can exercise self-compassion by reframing negative statements about yourself, into more realistic and encouraging ones. Use that same exercise to determine what brings you discomfort and to reframe those specific areas that create negative emotions in your life.

5. **Boundaries Regarding Physical And Mental Activities**

   Finally when it is time for your self-care routine, make sure that you are making this YOUR time, and that you are making the effort to block out any outside distractions. Apply the same rules with respect to your mental activities or personal projects and ensure that you are focused when engaging in these activities. Maybe you need to get down to writing that book you always wanted to write. Create a schedule that will reduce your time engaging in low-priority activities to accommodate your writing goals. Say no to other things that are least important and yes to those that are important!

Determining Your Limits and Setting Boundaries

It is not difficult determining what your limits are in all areas of your life with people, work, and social circles. Set some time aside to work through this exercise in your journal. You will reflect on your life and the quality of it to determine what makes you feel uncomfortable and the quality of all your associations with others.

1. Ask yourself: What causes you discomfort in each area of your life with regard to your association with people?

2. **Ask yourself:** Who gives you positive energy and what do you look forward to each day?

3. **Ask yourself:** What drains you and with whom do feel exhausted, negative, and unhappy?

4. Inside the circle write down what makes you feel safe, supported, and valued and with whom you feel this way. On the outside of the circle, write down everything that creates discomfort in your life. The things outside of the circle are what you need to avoid or limit as these things push the limits of your boundaries.

5. **Create boundaries:** Eliminate the discomfort so that you will not experience feeling uncomfortable, drained, used, or put on the spot anymore. Be very detailed, clear, and certain about the course of action you want to follow. Then implement these boundaries. (Hailey, 2022)

Key Takeaways

- Knowing what pushes you to your limits in all situations is just as important as eating healthy, exercising, or meditating daily.
- Address the stressors in your life that can be eliminated by setting healthy boundaries.
- Healthy relationships require healthy boundaries.

- Unhealthy relationships that do not have boundaries or limits will leave you feeling conflicted, resentful, and used.
- Identify all the things that create discomfort in your life in all areas to achieve clarity on where you need to create boundaries.
- Effective communication lies at the heart of boundary setting, and it usually reduces conflict in your life.
- Boundaries set us on a track that prioritizes you, and what is important to you.
- Ongoing discomfort in your life will continue to cause unnecessary stress and leave depleted, anxious, and negative.
- If you have always been an accommodating person to others at a high cost to your own happiness, then it is time to determine what your limits are.
- Do not betray yourself by agreeing to things that your heart is not invested in.
- As you transition to midlife, reducing stress, drama, and chaos and eliminating negative aspects of your life are important.

In the next chapter, you will come to terms with dealing with aging in a more positive way. It is ultimately your attitude and outlook that will determine how you feel about life and your prospects to experience joy, happiness, and personal liberation.

CHAPTER 12

SETTING YOURSELF UP TO BECOME THE BEST VERSION OF YOU

There is no greater freedom than knowing and accepting yourself. There is no other way to true happiness. –Marcee Martin

Being Older Does Not Mean That You Are Less Than What You Were

I know so many wonderful women who have lost their confidence as soon as they approach midlife. This is also why it was important for me to pursue this series. I've been there too, and I feel strongly that you can overcome any issues that you may be going through now related to midlife. You are here with me because we have something in common. We want our midlife years to be positively amazing. You need answers and are looking for a booster. I have them for you because I have walked in your shoes, and we are on the same journey. I remember all too well that dreaded feeling that stopped me in my tracks as I approached midlife. It stopped so many other women too in their tracks. Every woman goes through major changes, so you're not the exception.

Thankfully we have more information at our disposal now than women did 100 years ago. Living past 50 was a major milestone a century ago. Women had a much shorter lifespan back then so a majority of women did not make it to 50 (Druward, n.d). Thankfully, we have progressed in leaps and bounds and 50 is no longer the end of the road. You can now totally rock it at 50 and define new dreams for your life.

So start working through the layers that are keeping you stuck in negativity by doing the exercises set out here over the next 30 days. Go ahead and avoid procrastination. Make the changes in your life by following your heart and I promise you that soon you will be burying all those negative feelings in various secret places of the universe. You will heal and you will emerge resplendent, full of hope, love, and excitement.

It is Time to Let Go

I have realized that all those wonderful moments in my life called memories are what life is made of. I am thankful that I can be amazing now at midlife to implement a new lifestyle that supports this phase in my womanhood. It is time to let go of everything that has ever held you back before. Self-doubt is a thing of the past for me as it can be for you too. I live in the moment, fully present, vibrantly participating in this adventure called, LIFE. You can too and you shall.

Addressing the changes head-on by adjusting your mindset to embrace a growth outlook is a significantly positive step to take forward. Look within and connect with your inner child to emerge authentic. We must not neglect our inner child even at 50. There is a curiosity about the inner child that we can borrow as we begin our new midlife adventure. Be curious and take each day as a new opportunity to learn more about your emerging new self, as you heal and let go of the toxicity of the past. Here are some of the changes that usually bring us down that we need to overcome, to build up self-confidence, self-esteem, and self-acceptance:

Are you ready to live your best life now? Tell me how by writing below or you can also email me directly. If you would love to share with me details about your midlife struggles, then please feel free to contact me via email at this address: hello@marceemartin.com. I would love to hear from you about how this book has added value to your midlife journey. It would be wonderful to connect!

Physical Appearance

Yes, there is a slowing metabolism that some of us stress about. Keep in mind though that if you are overweight but it is not your goal to lose weight- that is okay. However, eating better is the better option to adopt for health reasons, especially given the inevitable falling estrogen and progesterone levels. As explained at length in Chapter 3 this state really defines some of the challenges you will face as a midlife woman. So whatever your goals or fears around physical appearance are now, remember that health is wealth.

It is not the twenties but you are most certainly not ancient either. Being healthy from the inside out at 50 can inspire you to go deeper with your wellness goals, beyond worrying about physical appearance or aging. Make sure that you prepare for those biological changes without negative baggage about this phase. Doing the work from the inside is more important than stressing over vanity goals to make an outward impression on people.

You've lived for a good few decades as a woman and you know how tiresome it is to adopt vanity goals to make an impression. Make changes that you are comfortable with, to support your physical, psychological, and spiritual health. This is where self-acceptance becomes crucial. Do take pride in looking and feeling great for yourself, so that you remain in a positively good mood when you step out the door in your own style that feels comfortable.

Psychological Changes

If you've never had a day's depression in your life, then you might be surprised as you approach midlife and move toward menopause. The mood swings that we discussed earlier will kick in and low and behold, you might be sad on some days. If the changes are having a major impact on your psychological health do seek professional help immediately to help reduce those symptoms and the impact.

In some cases, the psychological changes can lead to clinical depression, and it may require all of you to start working to get back to a healthier psychological state. However, if you follow a healthy self-care routine, do what you love, and ensure that you've addressed unresolved issues, you can then work out a plan for your career goals. If you keep moving forward with self-compassion, clinical depression will not manifest in your life. So chin up and once again, move more towards self-acceptance to rule out this possibility completely.

Career Changes

A sudden unexpected shift in your career or an inward striking desire to make a shift is not uncommon. Go ahead and examine new options. It is as good as taking an extended holiday. A recent study revealed that one in four women do consider a change of career during midlife (The Midlife Movement, 2014). Upskill and learn new things, it will keep your mind fresh. As long as you are enthused about the ideas that you have to spice up your career, you are moving in the right direction. Capitalize on your strengths and take a leap of faith with the right support, having weighed your options.

Thriving in a career that excites you and makes waking up every morning a new adventure will improve your sense of purpose, your self-esteem, and your self-confidence. This entire book is aimed at helping you find better coping skills to deal with the past, make peace with it, accept it, heal and learn from your earlier life experiences, let go of the toxicity, and get to a healthier, more inspiring psychological place in your life. Every chapter is building you to take you closer to a healthier place of self-acceptance, self-esteem, and self-confidence, all important ingredients for living a happier life.

Sweeping anything under the carpet that brings you the slightest degree of discomfort will rob you of being fully present in your life now. Instead, dealing with your past and bringing everything out toward the light of healing will help you to be anchored in the present. A strong transition to midlife does include: Putting the past to rest by honoring your journey, accepting everything that has happened in your life and honoring the changes that you are making now having acquired the wisdom of the ages. When we achieve this, we are making space to welcome new experiences, create new memories, and embrace a new journey. Claim your power of living in the now.

The Age Isn't the Problem: What You Think About The Age Matters The Most

I have learned that age is all in the mind. How you feel about your life and your prospects of living one that resonates with everything that is important to you is what truly matters. The biological changes are natural, as our physical bodies move from one biological phase to the next. The number of years we live on earth has everything to do with the natural biological process of aging. Honor that natural process without attaching labels that negate your individuality and inner youthfulness.

As women we all have unique issues to get through in life, however, we all want the same thing: happiness, peace of mind, and a positively inspiring life to feel good about. That is available to you. As you read earlier in the introduction, I too experienced being sucked into a whirlpool of negative emotions and spent a lot of my younger days being confused, feeling hopeless, and unsure of myself. Midlife comes as an awakening and once again it is our hormones that change things for us in midlife including our perspective. Thankfully too.

We can be younger in midlife and released from the negativity of the past if we choose to. An old adage comes to mind here: Youth is wasted on the young. Without a doubt one of the regrets we all experience at midlife is, "I could have done things differently if I knew then what I know now!" NOW is what we have and you and I both know better now what we should have known back then. Self-love is the elixir that will transform your life now if you embrace and accept the past as an important growth experience that was necessary to get you here now: The insightful phase of midlife.

Age is just a number. Maturity is what matters. Everything about life is what you make of it, including midlife. If you believe that you have lost the best days of your life and regret so many things it will feel like a wasted journey. However, if you learn to heal from the past and search for the hidden blessings you will see how worthwhile that journey was, even the challenges, setbacks, and tragedies that marked that journey. Everything is a gain and not a loss when you decide to make it count.

What you have learned in your journey is priceless, so honor it, even if some of the memories are not so pleasant, it is part of you. Rejecting any part of you is not loving because unless you value yourself, your whole self, the world will not value you. Authenticity is key to being valued. You deserve to be valued for the beautiful soul and woman that you are. However, remember that validation is important as long as it comes from within you, then it is a true reflection of self-love.

Your Attitude Is Everything

It is your attitude to menopause, midlife, and aging that will determine the quality of your next adventure, and how you thrive. Your attitude will also determine how you relate to the life ahead of you and the choices you now face. No one else on the planet is waking up dedicated to your life. Self-love is a game shifter. When you truly start loving and accepting yourself, you will start living your life to the fullest, and you will wake up enthused about a brand new day in front of you, a day that you can dedicate to what is important in your life.

There is no secret to enjoying midlife. There are only the facts: Love and accept yourself, practice self-care, do what you love, love what you do, and the world will be your oyster! Also, eat plenty of oysters (if you like them) to spice up your sex life, and talk about the wonderful changes that are taking your place in your life to others. Perimenopause and menopause are your destination. Embrace these changes lovingly. Your body needs nourishment, self-care, and love.

Your body has served you lovingly for so many years, and it needs you to love it and nurture it in new ways. Running away from the changes, and cringing at the thought of getting older will only keep you stuck in an unhealthy cycle of negativity, unhappiness, and loneliness. You deserve better. Spread your wings, change your lifestyle to accommodate midlife, and set yourself free instead.

Dealing With All Outstanding Issues Concerning Midlife Head-On

Congratulations for making it this far! You've made it to the final exercise in this book. In this exercise, we will go through a quick checklist to ensure that you are ready to start implementing all the changes you want to experience in midlife without the baggage of regret still hanging over your head like a dark cloud. I hope that you have worked through all the other exercises. If you haven't I strongly suggest that you do before attempting this exercise. Feel free to go back and read through each chapter and do the exercises, until you've emptied yourself of any regrets, worries, traumas, and negativity.

In your final exercise, you are going to do a lifestyle audit. Here's how to do it:

1. Reflect on every area of your life and write down what is working and what is not working. Meditate on how you can level up your game in those areas by reflecting on your next growth phase for all the things that are working.

2. Finally, reflect on the things that do not appear to be working out in your life and start brainstorming on how you can change that from today onwards. Remember that in order to make things work you need to be very honest with yourself. Take the gloves off and open up to yourself!

Commit to the changes you've highlighted, stick to them, be flexible at the same time, and be willing to make adjustments as you progress. Open your heart and be guided by love in all your efforts to improve your life. It does take some work to reach a stage of complete confidence in yourself, especially in midlife. Keep moving forward, and every step toward improvement adds up. However, as you already know, it is possible to own your best qualities and feel completely exuberant from the inside out, as you've learned from Theresa St. John, Sarah, Susan, and Alison's midlife transition success stories in this book.

My story is also a success story. Today, I completely own my personal space after doing the work necessary to heal and transform my life from the inside out. I am still loving every moment of this midlife journey of self-discovery. It is also wonderful being here helping you too along the way. However, to reach true liberation you do need to raise your level and totally commit to your own personal development. This is why my next book in this series is: The SELF CONFIDENCE workbook for MIDLIFE WOMEN: *A 30-Day Self-Discovery Journey to Own Your SH*T and Reignite the Badass Women That You Are.*

If you send an email to me now I can include you in my VIP mailing list to receive a copy of the second book before it is released to the public. Here is my email address: hello@marceemartin.com. Also, feel free to share with me details about your midlife struggles. I would love to hear from you. There's a lot more you can do to regain full confidence and completely release yourself from any toxicity that enters your sacred space. Anything and everything is possible if you are determined enough.

We are already confident as children, but as you know, the years do take their toll on us and we slowly move away from that natural inborn confidence. We face challenges that slowly chip away at our true nature. As you've already learned in this book, it doesn't have to be that way and a crisis of any kind is a red flag. A crisis says to us that we have neglected some aspects of ourselves that need healing and love. The next book awaits you and it will uplift you even further in your journey of midlife renewal. So get ready to rekindle your passion for life and success by mastering self-confidence in the next book!

Key Takeaways

- You can overcome any issues that you may be going through now related to midlife.
- Make sure that you work through the layers that are keeping you stuck in negativity.
- Do all the practical exercises set out in this book and work through the changes you need to implement in your life over the next 30 days.
- Addressing the changes head-on by adjusting your mindset to embrace a growth outlook is a significantly positive step in the right direction.
- Look within and connect with your inner child to emerge authentic, even at 50 curiosity will bring a new energy of excitement.
- Being healthy from the inside out at 50 can inspire you to go deeper with your wellness goals.
- Follow a healthy self-care routine, do what you love, address unresolved issues, work out a plan for your career goals, and keep moving forward with self-compassion and success is yours!

Marcee A Martin

- Midlife comes as an awakening and once again it is our hormones that change things for us in midlife including our perspective.

CONCLUSION

You've given it all you got! Well done for taking full command of your life during this important transition. It is a significant stepping stone towards fulfilling your true destiny: To be the amazing woman that you were born to be. Together we've journeyed through the years of your life, to uncover and remove the negative, toxic programming that set you up for anxiety, stress, depression, and personality issues. This negative mindset does occur by default most of the time, especially when you allow life to dictate to you the terms of your own happiness.

You can choose your reaction and response to midlife just as you do in all other situations. When you decide to choose your reaction wisely, growth will occur. Real meaningful psychological growth will occur and this is what your self-love journey has been about in this book. You aim should always be to transcend the limited fear-based thoughts, looking for those hidden blessings, and removing self-doubt.

Keep flipping that switch from negative to positive and soon you will have a completely new program in place in your subconscious mind, to replace the old negative patterns. Go back to read what you journaled here in your workbook and keep working with the insights and breakthroughs that you encountered in the process.

As you've learned, the new unknown territory of midlife is largely defined by hormonal changes, followed by other physical changes, psychological reactions, mood swings, hot and cold flashes, and many other side effects listed in detail in Chapter 3. All of these new effects of the midlife transition need adjustment, awareness, and a solid daily self-care routine in place to ensure that the blessings of midlife will outweigh any discomfort that you may experience. Just remember that you're now in full bloom. Embrace it and be enthused, it is a matter of adopting the right attitude toward yourself, midlife, and nature. Midlife is a natural transitional phase that women experience.

Only when negativity hardens into belief systems do we experience a crisis of some sort. There's only so much our loving hearts can handle. We are made for love, to grow and expand in awareness through all of the phases of our lives. From puberty to midlife it's been one incredible ride already! Now, at midlife, it gets better, and you can be all that you ever wanted to be and so much more. You've got the energy, willpower, and resilience to make the changes that are necessary to live the life you deserve to live. Self-love will set you free every day so don't even consider skimping on it and making sacrifices at the expense of your personal happiness.

Our journey has only just begun. The entire series I have created for midlife women will help you reclaim your power and happiness to achieve emotional stability. The series is designed specifically to take you all the way to the finishing line as a winner, as you come to grips with the crucial changes you are undergoing physically, psychologically, and spiritually.

This important new milestone in your life is worthy of fully embracing. We may be older and past what is considered our prime years, but I promise you that the best is still to come!

Get ready to take your midlife self-love journey to the next level. In this series, you will keep spreading your wings to reach new heights in personal growth, and achieve more insightful healing breakthroughs. I look forward to our next midlife coaching session in my book: Self-confidence Workbook for Midlife Women: A 30-Day Self-discovery Journey To Own Your SH*T and Reignite the Badass Women That You Are.

I also look forward to hearing from you personally. Send me an email, tell me what you think about my series, share your midlife stories, and let us connect, heal, and transform our lives together, to reflect our fullest and greatest potential. My email address again is hello@marceemartin.com. An honest review of my book will also be much appreciated: Let others know how you've benefitted and how they can too. Thank you sincerely for taking this journey with me. Until next time, keep shining!

ABOUT THE AUTHOR

Marcee calls herself the "happiest author" on Planet Earth. However, her journey to inner happiness was long, protracted, and often complex. In the end, it was fulfilling and it led her to a quest of helping midlife women navigate their lives to new inspired destinations. After suffering from years of low self-esteem, chronic anxiety, non-existent self-confidence, and a plethora of other emotional disorders, Marcee finally turned her life around.

Her breakthrough came when she was on the brink of a total mental and emotional breakdown. She searched through more than 200 books (across several niches) for answers, and insight into finding true happiness. She also watched more than 200 videos and attended many seminars and classes. Hitting rock bottom mentally and emotionally released Marcee's inner desire to improve her life in every way possible.

The secrets of human relationships and psychology unearthed in the research transformed her life and she never looked back. Marcee's life became a series of breakthroughs until she completely rebuilt and developed a new relationship with herself, learning all about self-love. This new relationship also improved her communication skills with other people. Marcee believes that everyone can communicate better if they know how to listen to others and read their body language.

In her own words, "I was born shy but I have come to realize that with the right approach, anybody can become a great conversationalist and a people's magnet. My life mission is to teach that approach." For the last five years, Marcee's new quest has been bringing other people closer to happiness through her books. The pillars of her teachings revolve around the following:

- Mindfulness and meditation techniques for anxiety, depression, and stress.
- The importance of listening (and not just hearing).
- Ways to challenge and fix cognitive distortions.
- The best ways to communicate even during difficult times.
- New methods to shape and discuss with your inner critic.
- CBT techniques for restoring emotional balance.
- The importance of self-love, self-esteem, and self-confidence.
- How to deepen empathetic traits without becoming codependent.
- Coaching to build conversational skills.
- Learning to develop charisma and using witty banter to great effect.
- Body language clues and how to read between the lines.

Marcee lives in New York City with her best friend (husband), and two cats!

Thanks for reading my book!

I am grateful that, from all the books on Amazon, you chose my book. It is my hope that you found great value in it.

Before you leave, can I ask a small fraction of your time? I'd like to ask you to leave me a **review on Amazon, or a star-rating**; doing so is immensely helpful for an independent author like me.

This is one way you can help me reach more people, to spread the word how this book can potentially help others.

Scan to leave a review:

$129 FREE

Achieve a Worry-Free Smile with these
12 Mental Health Books!

The Easy Way to Improve Mental Health

Therapy doesn't have to be so expensive and complicated. That's why we are giving you these 7 eBooks and 5 bonus workbooks so you can start improving your mental health right away, without leaving your home!

- **Stop Worrying All the Time**: Stop those nagging thoughts in their tracks with mindfulness and anti-anxiety tips expert CBT therapists use!

- **Do Therapy Your Way**: Start taking action with 5 BONUS workbooks, so you can start smiling, laughing, and enjoying life on your own!

- **Love Yourself, Love Others**: Enhance your career, relationships, hobbies, and more as you march through each day with confident self-esteem

Scan to download:

Loved this book? You may also want the other books in this series:

What others are saying:

Christina Forster
★★★★★ **Great book!**
Reviewed in the United States on January 31, 2023
Verified Purchase

This book is so helpful in learning about self-worth and self-esteem and different treatments to help. It was interesting reading about how self-doubt can creep in and start to cause a decrease in self-esteem and self-confidence. Certain things such as perfectionism can lead to self-doubt. I enjoyed learning more about CBT and how to use it to help with one's sense of self. CBT can help you overcome self-doubt. It is explained in a very easy to understand way. I really enjoyed the chapter on radical self-compassion. If we could all learn to be kinder to ourselves it would go a long way!

A D
★★★★★ **Improve your confidence**
Reviewed in the United States on January 30, 2023
Verified Purchase

If you are your own worst critic like me then this book can help. They provide positive psychology exercises and CBT worksheets to help you overcome your mind and silence your inner critics. You learn ways to reduce perfectionism. Explain the roots of self-doubt and provide exercises to work on understanding yourself worth. I love chapter 7 that gives exercises for radical compassion. By the end I gained useful tools to help me take more control of my life.

Daniela Hernández
★★★★★ **Healing book**
Reviewed in the United States on January 30, 2023
Verified Purchase

Unfortunately a few years ago I had a relationship that lowered my self-esteem and now I'm trying to start a new relationship with another person. However, my lack of self-esteem is affecting both of us. This book helped me heal many wounds and love myself over anything else.

Scan to check out books on Amazon
→

REFERENCES

Berman, R. (2020, July 16). *New study suggests we have 6,200 thoughts every day. Big Think.* https://bigthink.com/neuropsych/how-many-thoughts-per-day/

Cabrera, Dr. B. (2022, May 22). *A Positive Mindset Can Increase Longevity. Cabrerainsights.com.* http://cabrerainsights.com/?p=4578

Center, K. C. (2021, October 4). *Regrets After A Midlife Crisis: Make Peace With Your Past. Kentucky Counseling Center.* https://kentuckycounselingcenter.com/regrets-after-a-midlife-crisis-make-peace-with-your-past/

Chronic Stress Puts Your Health at Risk. (2021, July 8). Mayo Clinic; Mayo Foundation for Medical Education and Research. https://www.mayoclinic.org/healthy-lifestyle/stress-management/in-depth/stress/art-20046037

Contributor, T. O. (2020, January 17). *9 habits that can instantly destroy your reputation, according to these self-made millionaires. CNBC.* https://www.cnbc.com/2020/01/17/9-habits-that-will-instantly-destroy-your-reputation-according-to-self-made-millionaires.html

Depression: MedlinePlus Genetics. (2018, April 1). MedlinePlus. https://medlineplus.gov/genetics/condition/depression/

Dresden, D. (2022, October 12). Mood swings during menopause: Causes and treatments. www.medicalnewstoday.com. https://www.medicalnewstoday.com/articles/317566#symptoms

Drevitch, G. (2022, May 18). Midlife Depression in Women. Psychology Today. www.psychologytoday.com. https://www.psychologytoday.com/us/blog/counseling-keys/202205/midlife-depression-in-women

Durward, E. (n.d.). Menopause. Avogel https://www.avogel.co.uk/health/menopause/

E, S. (2020, June 18). How Will Oysters Help Increase My Libido during Menopause? Menopause Now. https://www.menopausenow.com/loss-libido/articles/how-will-oysters-help-increlease-my-libido-during-menopause

Globetrotter, M. (2020, January 2). My Emotional Upheaval at Midlife. Midlife Globetrotter. https://midlifeglobetrotter.com/emotional-at-midlife/

Globetrotter, M. (2021, January 3). Making Yourself a Priority at Midlife. Midlife Globetrotter. https://midlifeglobetrotter.com/prioritize-yourself/

Golden, B. (2019, January 12). How Self-Criticism Threatens You in Mind and Body. Psychology Today. https://www.psychologytoday.com/us/blog/overcoming-destructive-anger/201901/how-self-criticism-threatens-you-in-mind-and-body

Hailey, L. (2022, April 15). How to Set Boundaries: 5 Ways to Draw the Line Politely. Science of People. https://www.scienceofpeople.com/how-to-set-boundaries/

Harvard Health Publishing. (2014, July 16). What meditation can do for your mind, mood, and health. Harvard Health. https://www.health.harvard.edu/staying-healthy/what-meditation-can-do-for-your-mind-mood-and-health-

Helmer, J. (2021, December 15). Tai Chi and Qi Gong: Better Balance and Other Benefits. WebMD. https://www.webmd.com/fitness-exercise/a-z/tai-chi-and-chi-gong

Hot Flashes: Triggers, How Long They Last & Treatments. (2022, March 21). Cleveland Clinic. https://my.clevelandclinic.org/health/articles/15223-hot-flashes

How to cope with a midlife crisis. (n.d.). Mindtools https://www.mindtools.com/axp1cfk/how-to-cope-with-a-midlife-crisis

Increasing Estrogen Levels. (2020, June 18). SheCares. https://www.shecares.com/hormones/estrogen/increasing-estrogen-levels

Jacobs, D., & Ford, V. (2020). How to Master Menopause: Practical Guidance for Dealing with Hot Flashes, Weight Gain, Insomnia, Mood Swings, and Other Menopause Symptoms. Wise Media Group.

Jacobson, A. (2021, July 20). How I Learned to Love Myself in Midlife. Know Thyself, Heal Thyself. https://medium.com/know-thyself-heal-thyself/how-i-learned-to-love-myself-in-midlife-ae5d3f80a6db

John, T. S. (2014, September 2). How I Changed My Life Completely At Midlife. Better after 50. https://betterafter50.com/how-i-changed-my-life-completely-at-midlife/

Johnson, A. (2022, September 1). What are the 3 hormones released during exercise? Scienceoxygen.com. https://

scienceoxygen.com/what-are-the-3-hormones-released-during-exercise/

Kirilova, K. (2019, February 19). *6 Ways to Improve your Self-image and Mindset at Midlife.* Career Life Choices. https://careerlifechoices.com/your-self-image-and-mindset-at-midlife/

Earthing and Grounding: Science, Benefits, How to. (2022, March 3). Dr. Robert Kiltz. https://www.doctorkiltz.com/earthing-grounding/

Ladish, L. (2014, April 6). *What Really Matters In Midlife: Thriving.* Viva Fifty! https://www.vivafifty.com/midlife-priorities-women-234/

Lusinski, N. (2018, July 27). *11 Women On What Self-Love Means To Them.* Bustle. https://www.bustle.com/p/11-women-on-what-self-love-means-to-them-9910840

Menopause in China, How China Views and Treats Menopause. (2019, April 8). Vergo Woman. https://www.vergowoman.com/menopause-in-china/

Nine Benefits of Yoga. (2021, August 8). Hopkins Medicine. https://www.hopkinsmedicine.org/health/wellness-and-prevention/9-benefits-of-yoga

Nine Unusual menopause symptoms to look out for. (2021, December 15). Live Healthily. https://www.livehealthily.com/self-care/8-unusual-menopause-symptoms-to-look-out-for

Nollan, J. (2020, July 9). *8 Emotional Self-Care Strategies: Take Care Of Yourself Emotionally.* A Conscious Rethink. https://www.aconsciousrethink.com/13567/emotional-self-care/

Olivine, A. (2022, March 24). *8 Benefits of Therapy*. Verywell Health. https://www.verywellhealth.com/benefits-of-therapy-5219732

Perera, K. (2020, May 28). *The Importance of Self Acceptance*. More Self-Esteem. https://more-selfesteem.com/the-significance-of-self-acceptance/

Randolph, C. (2019, May 2). *Why Should We Care About Self-Development in Midlife? Inspire My Style*. Inspire my style. https://inspiremystyle.com/why-should-we-care-about-self-development-in-midlife/

Ready, B. (2012). *Aging and Emotions*. Psychology Today. https://www.psychologytoday.com/us/blog/your-quality-life/201208/aging-and-emotions

Risser, M. (2021, October 4). *11 Ways to Practice Emotional Self Care*. Choosing Therapy. https://www.choosingtherapy.com/emotional-self-care/

Schaaf, S. V. (2021, March 6). *Black women's health problems during menopause haven't been a focus of medicine. Experts and activists want to change that*. Washington Post. https://www.washingtonpost.com/health/black-women-menopause-hot-flashes/

Scott, E. (2008, May 9). *How to Deal With Negative Emotions and Stress*. Verywell Mind. https://www.verywellmind.com/how-should-i-deal-with-negative-emotions-3144603

Self-Love: The World Needs Us. (2018, February 1). Women Together. https://womentogether.com/lifenotes/article/love-campaign-powering-up-self-love/

Six Ways we can Lose our Confidence in Midlife & How to Rediscover it. (2014, May 14). The Midlife Movement.

https://www.themidlifemovement.com/blog/6-ways-to-rediscover-confidence-in-midlife

Social, S. (2022, March 9). *7 Ways To Practice Emotional Self Care*. Steph Social. https://stephsocial.com/2022/03/09/emotional-self-care/

Thirteen Habits of Self-Love Every Woman Should Adopt. (2017, November 17). Healthline. https://www.healthline.com/health/13-self-love-habits-every-woman-needs-to-have#1.-Stop-comparing-yourself-to-others

Thomas, A. J., Mitchell, E. S., & Woods, N. F. (2018). *The challenges of midlife women: themes from the Seattle midlife Women's health study*. Women's Midlife Health. https://doi.org/10.1186/s40695-018-0039-9

Thriving, E. and. (2022, September 24). *Self-Confidence Quiz – How Confident Are You? Empowered and Thriving*. https://empoweredandthriving.com/Self-confidence-Quiz/

Three Benefits of Meditation for Menopause Relief. (2020, July 14). Well-Balanced Women. https://wellbalancedwomen.com/3-benefits-of-meditation-for-menopause-relief

Thriving, E. and. (2023, February 5). *What Are Some Confidence Hacks? Empowered and Thriving*. https://empoweredandthriving.com/what-are-some-confidence-hacks/

Upshaw, W. N. (2020, March 24). *Signs You Are Experiencing Depression vs. A Midlife Crisis*. NeuroSpa. https://neurospatms.com/signs-you-are-experiencing-depression-vs-a-midlife-crisis/

What is Destructive Criticism. (2021, July 22). Pareto Labs. https://www.paretolabs.com/destructive-criticism/

Whitbourne, S. K. (2021, June 5). 7 Ways to Tell if Your Personality Is Bringing You Down. Www.psychologytoday.com. https://www.psychologytoday.com/us/blog/fulfillment-any-age/202106/7-ways-tell-if-your-personality-is-bringing-you-down

Wong, K. (2016, April 14). Why Self Care Is So Important. Lifehacker. https://lifehacker.com/why-self-care-is-so-important-1770880812

IMAGE REFERENCES

Adams, W. (2020). spa-relaxation-relax-massage-4962688. https://pixabay.com/photos/spa-relaxation-relax-massage-4962688/

Altmann, G. (2019). Self-love-heart-board-blackboard-3969679. https://pixabay.com/photos/self-love-heart-board-blackboard-3969679/

Altmann, G. (2018). Woman-presentation-poster-really-3271589. https://pixabay.com/photos/woman-presentation-poster-really-3271589/

Dannie. (2017). self-confidence-strength-wave-sea-2036236. https://pixabay.com/photos/self-confidence-strength-wave-sea-2036236/

Earth-hour-drawing-sustainability-4827744. (2020). https://pixabay.com/illustrations/earth-hour-drawing-sustainability-4827744/

Fazzeri, G. (2020). Women-laughs-party-wedding-5795442. https://pixabay.com/photos/women-laughs-party-wedding-5795442/

Friend, N. (2016). *yoga-woman-nature-landscape-1812695.* https://pixabay.com/photos/yoga-woman-nature-landscape-1812695/

Geissler, E. L. (2020). *Sunflowers-field-flowers-meadow-5482116.* https://pixabay.com/photos/sunflowers-field-flowers-meadow-5482116/

Hassan, M. (2020). *Woman-yoga-meditation-logo-light-5485664.* https://pixabay.com/vectors/woman-yoga-meditation-logo-light-5485664/

Lenin, S. (2017). *yoga-woman-lake-outdoors-2176668.* https://pixabay.com/photos/yoga-woman-lake-outdoors-2176668/

Marco, P. (2020). *Yoga-yoga-pose-asana-sunset-woman.* https://pixabay.com/photos/yoga-yoga-pose-asana-sunset-woman-5281457/

Silvia. (2017). *Dragon-woman-human-stone-pebble-2634391.* https://pixabay.com/photos/dragon-woman-human-stone-pebble-2634391/

Silvia. (2018). *Woman-dragon-relax-tame-fantasy-3613722.* https://pixabay.com/photos/woman-dragon-relax-tame-fantasy-3613722/

Tamay, O. (2018). *Starfish-woman-lady-person-people-3656896.* https://pixabay.com/photos/starfish-woman-lady-person-people-3656896/

Valentine-s-day-the-heart-of-people-1213612. (2016). https://pixabay.com/photos/valentine-s-day-the-heart-of-people-1213612/

Woman-meditate-balance-relax. (2020). https://pixabay.com/photos/woman-meditate-balance-relax-5594023/

Women-yoga-class-asana-fitness. (2016). Pixabay. https://pixabay.com/photos/women-yoga-class-asana-fitness-1178187/

Made in the USA
Las Vegas, NV
18 December 2023